CW01638048

Lectures on Raja Yoga by Sri Swami Chidananda.
David De Angelis 2017

Lectures on Raja Yoga

By

Sri Swami Chidananda

Table of Contents

Preface

Peace be unto all beings!

Adorations unto the Almighty Lord! Homage unto the great Sage Patanjali, the ancient expounder of the science of Raja Yoga! Salutations to Worshipful Master Gurudev Sivananda at whose Feet this book is offered in reverence and devotion!

I am happy to give this brief Preface to this little book on the subject of Raja Yoga edited by Sri Swami Vimalananda, who has been a devoted helper to me in innumerable ways over the past more than two decades.

The matter in this book comprises a series of class lectures given in Beirut (Lebanon) at the Yoga Shanti Niketan where I had been invited by the Founder-Director, Mrs. Louisa Raaff, known to her student circles as Mother Shanta and Mother Swami Lalitanandaji, who generously helped towards this trip. I went to Beirut and stayed for six weeks in the spring of 1973 fulfilling a programme of a series of class lectures, Satsangas, meditation sessions and public engagements.

Two other friends who took great interest in my visit and were very helpful to me are

Sri Omar Mansaur and Jean Pierre Sara, both spiritual seekers taking keen interest in Yoga practice and meditation. To these wonderful persons I owe a debt of gratitude and take this opportunity of recording it here.

I must also mention the young student, Panos Tsakalian of the American University at Beirut who arranged lectures at the University.

These lectures have been given in very simple language avoiding technical terms as far as possible. They are easy to understand as they were originally addressed to a group of persons who were strangers to Indian philosophical thoughts and the subject of YogaDarshana.

It was a new subject and the field was unfamiliar to their thought-form. As such, these talks were necessarily made simple for them to grasp. An orderly sequence was attempted at the time of their delivery.

Therefore, this arrangement makes the present volume something in the nature of a primary text-book on Patanjali Yoga. Hence it is felt that it may be of some value to beginners and would help them to get a preliminary knowledge of Ashtanga Yoga.

Whatever is helpful and of any value in this volume belongs to Maharshi Patanjali, to whom I pay homage.

Any discrepancies and shortcomings the reader may find belong to me. The entire project was undertaken in the spirit of Guru-Seva to Worshipful Master Swami Sivanandaji.

My many grateful thanks to each and everyone who has made this volume possible.

Swami Chidananda

First Lecture:

Raja Yoga is a Universal Science

Beloved Immortal Souls! Radiant Children of Light! Greetings to you all in the name of Yoga. Yoga, the ancient science of India, is the common heritage of humanity, though evolved in the East, though practised and expounded in India. This science of attaining universal consciousness is the common wealth of mankind. It is a science that goes beyond the barrier of any particular faith or religion, system or theology, and takes on the nature of spiritual process that is capable of being worked out within the interior of human consciousness irrespective of the personality. This consciousness, shines as the universal common denominator, as the common factor in all life. It runs as a subtle invisible cosmic link in all life, just as a thread runs as the common inner support through a necklace of beads of variegated colours, shapes and appearances, holding them all together, unifying them into one object, a necklace. Here is this Sutra or a thread, a unity within diversity.

Consciousness or the spiritual essence is similarly the unifying factor that underlies all forms in this universe that are apparent as different objects to our superficial, physical gaze. All such objects hold, within their apparent diversity, this inner Unity of Consciousness. The spirit within is the universal common denominator underlying all forms of existence, but it has become involved in mental processes, and through them got caught up within the meshes of sensual and physical nature.

Yoga presents a system of liberating the spiritual essence from this involvement, this entanglement in mental and physical processes. It achieves the effect of restoring the spiritual consciousness to its pristine state, its untrammelled, pure original state. The thesis of Yoga based upon the direct experience of those who became its expounders, is that your true nature, your real and essential nature, is pure bliss. It is pure peace. It is Ananda and Santi. Not sorrow. Not misery. Not grief. Not restlessness. Not agitation. Not tears. But peace and joy. Thus Raja Yoga is a scientific method of liberating the consciousness from the bondage of mind, senses and matter. It does not come into clash with any set of dogma or any specific religious belief. For, in the ultimate context, if you try to analyse religion to its gross roots, you will discover that all religions have as their ultimate aim, showing to the individual the path beyond sorrow, the way to supreme blessedness. Call it divine felicity, call it eternal beatitude, call it salvation, emancipation, liberation—the term which you use does not matter; the aim or the ultimate objective of religion remains the same. If you try to grasp the central essence of religion, the central spirit behind all the elaborate rituals and ceremonials, you will find that it is to bring man to God. And this Reality or this Cosmic Being called God denotes a state of perfection that transcends the imperfect experiences of this finite earth-life, that transcends sorrow and suffering. It denotes a positive state of perfect joy and peace.

Yoga therefore is a system, a science, a practice. Though it had its origin in India, though it was systematised by a people who professed the Vedic religion which we call Hinduism, Yoga is beyond religion and occupies a place in the spiritual life of man which is the common meeting ground of all humanity and has come down to us in this 20th century as a part of the universal heritage of mankind.

The Nature Of The World

Yoga, by itself, is a term that implies the bringing to an end man's involvement in sorrow and suffering. The life of man here in this universe is characterised by experiences which he does not like, experiences which are painful, experiences which he seeks to avoid but discovers by the time he approaches the end of his life that they are unavoidable. These are part and parcel of what we call earthly life here. Pain, sorrows and sufferings of various kinds seem inevitable and yet man all over the world tries to avoid suffering and sorrow, pain and misery, and tries to obtain, somehow or the other, a state of joy, of happiness. In this, man fails. He has failed in this ever since the dawn of creation. Not so much because this state of absolute transcending of sorrow and experience of absolute bliss does not exist, but merely because he searches for it in the wrong direction. He looks for it in the outer world, in objects. And no wonder he fails to find the perfect and absolute experience of joy there, because finite things, changeful things, perishable things, imperfect in their very nature, have a beginning and an end; they are conditioned in time and space. These things naturally cannot give perfect experience, because these things are fragmentary. Everything is relative. Everything is one of a pair of opposites. And our relationship, our contact, with all things is also short-lived. All coming together ends in going apart, and over and above this, that very instrument through which man has to relate himself to all things here is characterised by much imperfection.

What is that instrument through which man relates himself to this external world? The body with the five senses is that instrument. And that primary instrument through which the dweller within has to contact and perceive this phenomenal world is itself defective. It has a birth and ultimately goes to extermination in death; all the five senses through which it perceives the universe gradually fail when disease comes and gradually destroys them. If disease does not destroy them, the natural process in old age makes them weaker. Eye-sight weakens, hearing fails, limbs become feeble, and all the senses gradually grow cold. Thus the body suffers its natural characteristics of birth, growth, change, disease, old age, decay and death. Numerous other factors also torment this body—factors beyond the control of man—you have natural calamities like earthquakes epidemic and famine. Then war, revolution, wicked people, malarious mosquitoes, yellow fever, consumption, T.B., cancer, venereal disease, dysentery, cholera *ad infinitum.* Then there are natural calamities like the fury of the elements, cold wave, heat wave, drought, either too much rain or no rain, typhoons, hurricanes and blizzards.

Then there are those other afflictions which are man-made and also coming from various kinds of creatures and as though these miseries are not enough, from within one's own nature there arise factors that torment and destroy the peace of the human individual. Anger, hatred, jealousy, envy, frustration, disappointment, failure to achieve one's objective, fierce passion in the form of lust and greed—these fires in the human being inflame his mind, torment his heart and disturb his peace. How much of the ills of man come from his own inner psyche! The various agitating conditions upon which he has no control, the various cravings, desires, ambitions and urges which constantly keep the mind in a state of turmoil—a little of this inner inferno has been perceived and touched upon by Western psychologists.

So, elements beyond one's control, other forms of life outside oneself and factors within oneself—all these afflict man in addition to the inevitable fate of the body. Thus, real happiness or joy seems to be an ever-receding horizon and its contrary seems to be an all-too-immediate ever-present reality; and thus, man's quest for escaping, avoiding or overcoming pain and suffering and entering into a state of joy seems to be a wild-goose chase, seems to be a futile pursuit doomed to failure. And hopeless seems the quest of man for happiness. It is precisely in this area of man's aspiration, in this area of life's quest that the science of Yoga becomes relevant to all of us. It becomes very significant and meaningful and very important, for it emphatically declares that despite the deplorable fact that sorrow is the nature of this temporary earthly existence, the destiny of man is supreme joy. That is the thesis of Yoga. That is the emphatic declaration of Yoga. Man is made for the attainment of supreme joy and this supreme joy or perfect state of bliss is not to be a post-mortem attainment, is not to be an after-death state of being, but it is something that is capable of being attained here and now. And if man would claim his birth-right, it is within the reach of every human individual to attain to this perfect experience right here, even while dwelling in this body, in this very life.

The Purpose Of Yoga

The purpose of Yoga is to try to restore to man his pristine state of perfect bliss; and this it does by liberating the human individual from his involvement in body, senses and mind. This involvement itself is the prime cause for keeping him away from itself, is the greatest obstacle to his attainment of that experience which the Yoga science says lies right here, present at this moment. To become liberated from the bondage of pain, thus bringing to an end the union of man's nature with pain, is Yoga. How is this cessation of pain brought about by uniting the consciousness with that which is of the nature of Bliss? And that factor which is of the nature of pure bliss is called the Self; is called Brahman; is called God; is called Allah; is called Isvara, the Thing-In-Itself, Ahuramazda. It is the Deity. It is the Universal Soul, the Cosmic Reality, the Eternal Divine Principle which is the Alpha and Omega of all beings, which is the origin and fulfilment of this and all that exist. To bring into a state of oneness with it, relate yourself to it and achieve a perfection of relationship with it, is Yoga. And to achieve this end, you will have to carefully withdraw your involvement in the passing, the finite, the limited, the noneternal. This is a condition, is a prerequisite. Yoga teaches both—how to sever your connection to the non-eternal and how to enter into that connection to the eternal, the all-perfect, the infinite. Yoga teaches that both these aspects are two in one, that is, uniting yourself with the Divine and thus attaining the Bliss which you seek in vain in finite, earthly objects. That is Yoga. That is the purpose of Yoga. The process of Yoga is the turning away from that which is characterised by sorrow, by pain and which is perishable, destructible in its nature.

The Fourfold Path

This process of turning away from the finite, from the imperfect, the temporary, the passing and entering into a conscious connection with the Eternal, with the Divine, sums up the process of Yoga. How this can be done? Is there only one way or are there many ways? The answer to this is both. There is only one way, and there are many ways. And why this dual answer? There is only one way in the sense that all Yoga is movement towards the Divine, movement towards the Infinite, movement of the personal towards the Impersonal, of the individual towards the Universal, movement of man towards God. So, there is only one Yoga. But then, this movement can be accomplished through several levels of the human personality. This Godward movement, movement towards the Divine may be initiated and carried out through one of other, or, one or more of the powers, of the capacities, of the faculties that you possess. And depending upon which one of the faculty you make use of as a medium for bringing about Godward movement, movement towards the Reality, depending upon that faculty Yoga assumes a particular pattern and derives a particular name.

If you do this movement through philosophical speculation, you make use of your intellect and your power of reasoning as the medium of attaining the knowledge and experience of that Reality by diverting your consciousness as expressed through intelligence. Then you are a philosopher and the Yoga becomes what is known as Jnana Yoga, Jnana Yoga of the Vedanta Philosophy. And, instead of the intellect, if you make use of your feeling, your love potential, your ability to love, to exercise affection, devotion, sentimental and emotional aspect—this potential as your medium, then it becomes what is known as the Yoga of devotion or the path of love or Bhakti Yoga. And if you make use of the power of your thought, power of the mind, will to urge your entire inner being to resolutely move towards God or the Universal Consciousness, determined that you will not allow your mind to be divested or distracted in any way, then you become a Raja Yogin or the mystic who treads the path of contemplation, concentration and meditation. But in all these methods, though they make use of one or the other faculties that you are endowed with, they seek to work out the self-same process, the one identical movement. Therefore, Yoga is one in spite of being different according to the medium of your movement.

Why this movement? The single reason that God did not create man from the assembly line. God did not create him as a stereo-type. There are diverse temperaments. There is diverse nature, and also, some time diverse inclinations. One is inclined towards a particular path; even one's nature has a balance of all these three ingredients in equal proportion, mind and will, intellect and rationality, devotion and love. Yet, by one's inclination one may have a tendency towards one particular path. To suit all temperaments, all capacities and different tastes, diverse forms of a single, identical approach have been evolved in the ancient land of Yoga, without doing violence or altering the central fact of the spiritual essence, meeting needs arriving out of the diversity of human nature and taste. And among various paths, three main paths are just now mentioned. Approach through the intellect and rationality is Jnana Yoga, approach through devotion and love is Bhakti Yoga, and approach through mind and will is Raja Yoga.

In India, these different paths are based upon certain original source scriptures, certain definite authority, scriptures that were brought into being by those who had experienced the Reality. They were people who had not only experienced the Reality, but had become established in that Reality Consciousness permanently. So, they were adepts, they were perfect beings, the Masters of Wisdom. And they have left for the benefit of posterity, their Wisdom and hints about the methods in brief aphorisms. They are just hints and pointers. These aphoristic teachings have a certain logical unity. So, they formed one successive logical field of utterances making up one whole system. Therefore, they are called Sutras. Sutra is a thread that tied together, linked together. So they are not haphazard. These great Sutras are the Brahma Sutras, the most authoritative of all sources of aphorisms for the Vedantin or Jnana Yogin, the one who follows the path of knowledge; and the Bhakti Sutras of two great sages, Narada and Sandilya, the basic authority source for the expounding of the path of devotional philosophy.

The Nature Of The Mind

And then, the Yoga Sutras of the great sage Patanjali, which expound the system of mental discipline and the technique to turn the mind away from the passing phenomenon and to direct it towards the permanent reality. And it is these Yoga Sutras of Patanjali that we are concerned with. As I mentioned, the central thesis is the Yogic vision of man, Yogic knowledge of man's reality. Though apparently a physical creature and a mental personality, man is in reality a spiritual entity. That spiritual entity is of the nature of Perfection and Peace. It is the mental personality that keeps depriving the individual of an experience of one's real spiritual Reality. That spiritual Reality which is of the nature of pure Bliss is veiled over by the mind-stuff; and the mind-stuff being constantly in a state of unceasing activity, holds the consciousness of man in its grip. Thus, the human individual is ever conscious of himself as one or other of the moods of the mind and never conscious of himself as he always is apart from the mind, because of his constantly being involved in the ceaseless activity of the mind. So, the consciousness of human individual is either that 'I am thinking', 'I am feeling', 'I am seeing', 'I am hearing', 'I am tasting', 'I am touching', 'I am smelling', or 'I am sleeping', 'I am remembering', 'I am disapproved', or 'I am dissatisfied', 'I am in need', 'I am hungry', 'I am humiliated'—in this way, one is always aware of oneself as being something or other in relation to the mind and never apart from this involvement in the mind. This is the problem. And the sage Patanjali shows the way up, tackling the mind successfully in the light of his deep knowledge of the mind.

Now, the European modern psychologists also have entered into the study of the mind. They also have discovered the vagaries of the mind, different states of the mind that give rise to lot of imbalance and disturbance and which make man miserable and ultimately even bring about physical symptoms, give rise to various physical struggling to prescribe various methods of trying to free himself from these conditions based upon their knowledge of this human interior mind and its vagaries; but with what results! More psychological tests, more psychologists, more psychoanalysts, more psychiatrists, but more psychoses and more complexes. These have not solved any problem, but have only expounded man's knowledge of the problems. So everyone knows now that there is this complex, there is that complex, there is this obsession. Man is not anywhere near to a solution. What may be the reason for this? It is Patanjali who will tell you. Because, all those solutions that the psychologists are trying to formulate and find out, prescribe and work out, still lie within the realm of the mind. The main thing has not been achieved. If there are a hundred problems of a prisoner inside a jail, and the superintendent of a jail or the minister of prisoners or the jail-wardens thought out various solutions for the problems of the prisoner, but all are within the four walls of the jail. So, the prisoner is still a prisoner. He continues to be a prisoner. So you may just treat the trouble just like the modern medication. If there is an ear-trouble, he puts some antibiotics and suppresses it there. It is only shifting the pain or changing its outer shape and it only takes on a different appearance. In the same way, all essence of psychology to correct psychological ills within the framework of the mind, has its fate. Because, the prime cause of all these problems, of all these states, is the mind. Unless and until you formulate a method which will try to take you beyond the mind, as long as the mind and its limitation exist, mind-reactions exist. It will always manifest its nature. There is no stopping it.

The Psychology Of Yoga

The Yoga of Patanjali formulated a means by which the sum total of the very nature of the mind was checked. Mind in all its various manifestations was mastered through a set of disciplines, a system of disciplines by which he arrived at a state of mindtranscendence. He had the advantage over the Western psychologists. In the entire study of modern Western psychology, specially the modern psychology as started by recent psychologists, you will find that the genesis of this science is based upon the study and observation of an imbalanced mind. It was morbid psychology actually. The study itself arose from this morbid, abnormal mind. Whereas in the case of Patanjali and the ancient seers, they took for their study, not the abnormal mind, they took for their study not even the human mind, not even the mind which has already become individualised in the human personality, already become conditioned by the human personality and assumed a finite shape, but they made their study of the mind-principle as such, the original mind-principle, the cosmic mind-principle as such. So, they went into a study of the mind-stuff as it was. It is here that you have to go into the cosmology, coming into the projection of this manifest universe, evolved from the Unmanifest. So, among many things that were evolved, grosser things like the five elements—the earth, fire, air, water, ether—and the five different kinds of forces in nature took the form of the universe, and the mind-stuff, the universal mind-principle. As such, they entered into a study of mind in itself, the mind-principle as it was originally, not when it became a human mind, the finite mind, conditioned by personality. No. So they have this advantage—studying the mind as it was. They discovered certain basic features of the nature of the mind, and based upon this knowledge of the nature of mind, they formulated a system of overcoming it, mastering it. Basing the studies of this knowledge, they evolved a system of Yoga.

Firstly, that the mind-stuff by itself is centrifugal. It always goes out. Its tendency is extroverted, Bahirmukhatva. It is its first nature. Secondly, the inveterate nature of the mind-stuff is to get hold of name and form, of some objects. It cannot be by itself. It has always to assume the name and form of some object. This second inveterate nature of the mind is called objectification. They call it in Sanskrit as Vishayakara Vritti. It always takes the form or Akara of Vishaya or something. It has always to think of something. And the third inveterate tendency which Patanjali tells about the mind is that it does not stay content to assume the form of one thing and keep on to it. It has the inveterate tendency of constantly wanting to move from one thing to another. It cannot stick to one object, and so, Nanatva, multifariousness, the tendency of constantly jumping from one object to another. So, these are the three basic tendencies of the mind, outgoing tendencies of the mind. They are objectification, multiplicity and multifariousness. No wonder, endowed with these tendencies in the mind, you are totally deprived from the experience of the Self. Why? These three contradict the basic nature of your true reality, of the Self within. Because, the Self is the very innermost centre of your being from which the mind constantly draws the consciousness away, out.

Secondly, the Self is not an object of perception. It is the perceiver of all that is perceived. It is the Seer of all things that are seen. It is the Supreme Subject. It is that, that which is connoted by 'I', not of this or that, the very opposite of multifariousness. Mind, therefore, catching the consciousness of our human interior draws it forth outside. It revolves it in objects and scatters it among the many. Thus it effectively prevents the consciousness from moving within and resting in its original state as the unaffected, untouched, impartial Seer and finding its oneness, a total freedom and liberation from all distraction. So, this is the problem. Raja Yoga gives you this, stage by stage, methods of transforming the nature of the mind, and overcoming it. You see this duality. The Self is the innermost from within. The Self is the Supreme Subject and the Seer, and It is of the nature of non-dual consciousness. Mind is ever going outside, ever objectifying itself, thinking in terms of things and ever scattering itself amongst the countless objects of this universe. What are the disciplines and how Patanjali moves towards the successive solutions of these problems. It is a beautiful subject. We will take it up Monday night.

What are the various ways in which the mind manifests its activity of the outgoing nature? How to overcome them? What is the method or the discipline according to

Patanjali? What are the obstacles to these methods? What are the different solutions to these obstacles? How to counter these obstacles and successfully enter into the state of Self-experience? That will be our subject of consideration for Monday evening.

Second Lecture: Value of Raja Yoga

Beloved Immortal Soul! Radiant Atman! Greetings to you all again in the name of my holy Master Swami Sivananda. We had the first talk on Friday and this is the second talk. Before I make a review of what ground we covered on Friday, I would once again like to tell you that the specific motive with which I am speaking to you, the objective with which I give these classes, is not so much to provide you with an academic knowledge of the subject. That also, of course, you will acquire during the course of these talks. But, much more than that academic knowledge, you gain the greater purpose. The more important approach with which these talks are given, is that they may be able to help you fight now in overcoming some of the difficulties and problems you have in your life, in your own efforts to bring about a certain harmony and balance and equipoise within your own personality, in your efforts at acquiring certain degree of self-governance, certain degree of control over your own inner being, mind, its thoughts, its desires and its various tendencies, so that to that degree and extent to which you will apply the knowledge you will get during these talks, to that degree and extent, your life may become enriched, your life may gain something in terms of more clear understanding of what is going on within you. You may also be put into possession of certain fundamental truths, lacking the knowledge of which the individual is bound to come to grief again and again, is bound to be caught in the net of sorrow, suffering and grief, and gaining the knowledge of which one could definitely, to an appreciable degree, liberate oneself from avoidable suffering and grief. It won't be either an exaggeration or a frivolous statement, if one said that to some extent, in some way, Raja Yoga enables the person to be one's own psychiatrist, enables the person to one's own psychological counsellor, so that he need not have to go to some one else to help him to overcome his problems. You become capable of helping yourself to overcome many of your problems. Because, the key of overcoming problems is understanding the problems. As long as you do not understand a problem in its proper light, you are confused. But once you understand, it becomes simple, it becomes clear. You are no longer confused. Your way is clear. You know what to do. This is the value of Raja Yoga. And more than anything else, the specific intention here is to put into your hands or into your possession certain facts, certain new information and basic knowledge about the inner dimension of your being. You can be helped here and now. It is pragmatic. It is practical.

The immediate intention of giving these talks is that you may be put into possession of a clear understanding of many of the new unclear areas of your own interior being, your mind and its activity. Therefore, I wish also that you will listen and try to attend to these talks in the same approach, looking it at the same angle—in what way it is going to help me? In what way I can make use of this knowledge? In what way I can apply it in my life immediately? Not merely have the satisfaction of feeling that now I know what Raja Yoga is, I have had an exposition of Patanjali's Raja Yoga Sutras, and so, I have got some knowledge about the higher Yoga, not Hatha Yoga, but the inner Yoga. Now, it is not merely to give you this satisfaction, but more to provide you with a knowledge that can be applied immediately, and an understanding which will be of immense pragmatic value, and over and above that, to give you an academic knowledge of what this science tells you and what Yoga is. In this consideration, last time, we briefly touched upon some of the broad aspects of Yoga itself. What is the meaning of Yoga? What is the purpose of Yoga? What is the process of Yoga? How does it help man?

Yoga, The Essence Of World's Religions

Yoga is the fundamental Universal essence of the world's religions, isolated from its specific framework and presented in the most general terms so as to be acceptable to human beings all over the world, no matter what the religious belief or what particular faith one belongs to. Yoga does this by going to the innermost spiritual depth of man and by-passing the rituals and ceremonials, superstructure of practical religion. It has formulated and presented a method by which the spirit of the human individual can liberate itself from its involvement in matter and in the material world of sense-objects, its involvement in mind and the interplay of the mind-activities. The spirit is restored back to the pure experience of its Self in its positive, untouched state. We saw how the basic thesis of Yoga is that this innermost spiritual nature of yours is of the nature of Bliss, is of the nature of absolute, perfect joy. Once you are united into the pure experience of your pristine real nature, you are in a state of Bliss. All religions have as their ultimate aim, giving to man this highest experience of perfect Bliss. They call it beatitude, felicity; call it salvation, call it God-experience, call it heaven.

The aim of all religions is to show man the path beyond sorrow and pain, and to show him the way to Bliss, to show him the way to supreme Blessedness, a perfect experience of absolute joy. They are described variously in different theological terms and scriptural languages. But there is an essence of the aim of religion, and Yoga has merely done this great service to mankind and systematically taking him through certain definite processes. Whereas the religions have tried to give it in a generic way, Yoga has scientifically systematised these processes of going beyond sorrow and entering into a state of absolute perfection, Bliss. Yoga liberates our inner spiritual Consciousness from its bondage to the outer sense-world and restores it to its pristine state. This true Selfexperience, Raja Yoga emphatically declares, based upon the personal experience of Seers. It emphatically declares that this Self is of the nature of absolute Bliss.

Yoga Is The Path To Bliss

Yoga is the path to Bliss. It is the essence of all religions, because the fundamental aim of all religions is to take man beyond sorrow to a state of supreme blessedness, of beatitude and perfection. Thus Yoga is a quest after the Eternal, the Permanent, the Infinite. That which hampers man's effort to move towards this Bliss, is his involvement in the non-eternal, in the finite world of objects, in the impermanent, involvement in mind and body, in the way of experiencing Self-consciousness; and therefore, Yoga is the process of turning away from the non-eternal and diverting of the personality potential of consciousness towards the Eternal.

How Yoga does it? We saw that it takes the help of whatever powers that are available to you, the power to feel, the power to think and reason, and the power to concentrate or the power to fix your mind upon a particular object. When you invoke the power of reasoning and make that the channel of your movement towards the Eternal, then you are a Jnana Yogin, you are a philosopher, man of wisdom. When you make use of the power to feel and try to divert your consciousness through devotion, love for God, then you are a Bhakti Yogin or the follower of the path of devotion and love. When you invoke the power of the mind to think intensely, to focus itself steadily upon that one Reality and enter into a state of absorption in that continuous, unbroken, focusing your mind, fixing your mind there, then you become the follower of meditation. This is Raja Yoga.

Study Of The Human Mind

Western psychologists studied the human mind, the individualised mind of man. Whereas the formulators of Yoga Science based their science upon their knowledge of their mind as such, as one of the cosmic principle, mind as one of the factors that became manifested during the course of cosmic projection. When the Unmanifest becomes manifested, It assumed innumerable names and forms. One of the factors that came into manifestation is the mind-principle. That was the state in which it was studied, and based upon a knowledge of the mind-principle as such, we saw among other things, that the mind principle is characterised by the outgoing tendency, the objectifying tendency and multifariousness, constant fritting from one object to another. It never remains upon any single object. We saw how the inevitable tendency of the mind-stuff was the direct contradiction of the Self. Self is the innermost reality, whereas the mind is outgoing in its tendency.

The Task Before Yoga

The Self is of the nature of Supreme Bliss. It is not an object of conception. It is the Subject. Therefore, the constant objectifying tendency of the mind came in the way of the subject dwelling upon the

Self—going back to its own inner pristine nature, original nature, original state of Consciousness, subjective state of Consciousness. The constant dispersal of the mind amongst the many, the multifarious objects, was the contradiction of Self-experience. Because, the Self is of the nature of non-dual Consciousness. It is one. It is the Universal Principle. It unifies all lives into one, homogeneous, non-dual oneness, unity. Fragmentation is the tendency of the mind. So, total reversal of the mind-nature in its constant manifestation in these activities, externalised modes of activities, constant objectification, constant assuming of names and forms, dwelling and acting in terms of names and forms, this oscillation and fickleness, has to be totally countered. They have to be overcome. They have to be blazed by the opposite. The mind has to be turned inward, and trained to remain as a subject, and also has to be made to focus itself upon one and not the many. This is the task before Yoga. As long as this state is not achieved, it is not possible to experience the Self. Because, when consciousness is involved in mental activity, it moves away from the Self, and consciousness involved in mental activity, itself becomes the basis of your earth-experience, your various mental states.

When the consciousness is thus involved in mental activities, you have joy and sorrow, pleasure and pain. Because, then you are caught in duality. The mind swings always from one object to the other. It is impossible to avoid it, as long as your consciousness is caught and held up within the mind-frame. Mind-activity and mind cannot be separated. Mind is what the mind does. When mind ceases to act, there is no mind. For, the entire range of human experiences is a question of activity of the mind. The moment the mental activity ceases, all activities come to an end. Therefore, they say there is no mind apart from thought. It is something which you have to reflect and try to grasp the subtle meaning of it. How do you know that when thoughts totally cease, there is no mind? Again, how do you know that when there is no mind, there is no experience?

Mind And Thought Are Inseparable

Both these questions are answered for you everyday, but you have not cared to perceive the answer. You have not cared to realise the significance of this answer. Is it possible for the mind to cease these activities, and if the activities cease, how do you know that all experiences also are put an end to? The answer to this comes to you not from outside but it springs up from within your own personal experience. This answer keeps on recurring to the human individual regularly, unfailingly in the cycle of 24 hours. And this deepest personal experience brings home to you the truth that mind is not apart from thought. There is no mind apart from thought. And by the cessation of thought for the time being, you overcome all experience, you cancel all experience. This experience is given to each human individual, every time during the total cessation of all his mental activity. You go into a state of deep sleep every night all the days of your life. When you enter into deep sleep, mental activity ceases so completely, to such an extent that even your self-awareness is no longer there. Your awareness of the universe, the world outside, is no longer there. You have no problems. You have no problems of either love or hatred. You have no problems either of anxiety or tension. You have no problems either of fear or worry. You have no problems either of bondage or any restrictions of your personal liberty. Because, the whole universe is cancelled, totally faded out of your experience, faded out of your consciousness, the moment you enter into deep sleep state. Because, that deep sleep state is characterised by the cessation of active thought.

The mind assumes the thought of nothingness. So the universe is annihilated and therefore, all experiences that come to the human being normally from the objects of the universe, from people, from sense-objects, are cancelled. Neither are you aware of yourself. You don't know whether you are a man sleeping or a woman sleeping. You don't know whether you are a child sleeping or an old person sleeping. You have no consciousness of human personality either; whether you are a god sleeping or a human being sleeping, you don't know. There is a total silence. Is this condition consciously brought about? The unfortunate thing is that it is not consciously brought about. Some mysterious force pushes you into it, and the same mysterious force pushes you out of it again into the conflict of life.

The second defect in this wonderful state into which you go is that though it immediately liberates you from all worries, fear, anxiety, tension, love and hatred, passion and all these things, when you come out of this state the next day, you are no better than what you were before you went into it. You come back the same person with the same attitudes, with the same ignorance, with the same folly. You are no wiser, no better. Therefore, you are once again subjected to the same torments of all the past previous days and the future. That is the defect of this state. The science of yoga tells you clearly that this is also a mental condition.

The Value Of Sleep

Sleep also is a mental condition. Sleep also is one of the states of the mind, a state of entering into the holding on to the thought of nothingness. Otherwise, it would be perfect. If you are transformed into that condition, when you wake up, you wake up as a sage or a seer or a person of wisdom or illumination. Then it would be grand. But the value of this state is; that it answers your two questions. When thought ceases, mind is no longer present. Because, if the mind is present then you must be able to see the whole world. When the mind is active, it functions through the five senses. It hears, sees, tastes, touches and smells, and perceives the external universe. If the mind is active and present, you can say 'I am'. In sleep you do not say 'I am'. Even the awareness of one's own self is annihilated. It is not there. Therefore, mind is absent when it ceases to function. When thoughts come to an end, mind is absent. It resurrects in the morning. But during the temporary state of sleep, there is a temporary annihilation of the mind. It sinks, it sets. There cannot be any mind apart from thought. There is no perception when thought-activity of the mind is annihilated or ceases to be. This is one answer you get and this answer gives you knowledge of your mind. And the second answer is that when thus with the cessation of thought, mind ceases to be, experience ceases, you are liberated from all experience. But that liberation is not permanent. That is the only flaw.

But this valuable knowledge of the mind is gained, mind is not apart from thought. When thought ceases, all experiences are cancelled and this leaves the working ground for the practices of Yoga.

Mental Activity Hides Your Real Nature

If we can consciously overcome the activity of the mind and control it, master it and totally subdue it then we can rest in a permanent state where all experiences are overcome. They are negated, and in that state of a conscious cessation of mental processes, you can attain to a state of perfect peace, perfect rest, perfect silence. Thus when the state of absolute silence of the mind is attained, whatever is beyond the mind becomes manifest. It now prevails in a field of your experience. Consciousness becomes characterised not by the experience of mental state, but consciousness becomes characterised by the experience of the Self, your true Self. For, there is nothing to obstruct. There is nothing to bar it or prevent it. When consciousness is characterised by mental activity, this mental activity becomes, as it were, like a cloud in front of the sun. Sun is there. When the cloud comes in front of it, it cannot be seen. Light goes away. Shadow comes. Or, upon the surface of an absolutely placid lake, you can see the bottom, the pebbles at the bottom clearly. But, if the surface is agitated, if it is made into ripples, then you cannot perceive clearly the bed of the lake. In the same way, the inner basis of your being is your Self. That is the Reality. That is of the nature of peace and joy. But, if that which is covering it, if it is in a state of constant agitation, activity, the substratum cannot be seen clearly. It appears to be agitated also, because of its association with the covering medium, the mind. Mind is the agitator of the surface of the lake of human consciousness and this consciousness is a part of the Divine Consciousness and it is of the nature of Bliss. So, they entered into It through the study of different ways in which mind-activity is constantly kept up.

The Dynamics Of The Mind

What is this mind dynamism? They perceive that this mind dynamism, constantly characterised in the waking state of the human individual consciousness is basically, fundamentally fivefold. The moment you open your eyes, you see things. I put my hand;

I immediately know cold or hot, whether it is soft or rough. The moment I open my eyes I see this wall whether it is grey, green, yellow, red or blue. The moment I listen, immediately I know, I begin to have knowledge whether I am hearing a motor car passing or a jet plane passing or some one speaking or a bird is cooing or leaves are shaking in the breeze. Mind is constantly, all the 24 hours, every moment of its waking consciousness, knowing things by seeing, by hearing, by tasting, by feeling and by smelling. So, this process of knowledge through perception is one of the inveterate continuous activities of the mind. This is simple. Later on, it is more complex also.

Secondly, another activity of the mind is wrong knowledge, perverted knowledge. This is also a knowledge, but you see it in a wrong way. You mistake a friend for an enemy, or mistake an enemy for a friend. It gives rise to various things. It gives rise to fright and wrong reaction. You mistake this external universe for something very permanent. You mistake it to be a likely source of your happiness. 'I will be happy if I get this object'. 'O, I am alone'. 'I am unmarried'. 'I have no companion'. 'If only I have a nice partner, if I fall in love and had a wife, if I fall in love and had a husband, then I will be happy'. So think man and woman. And then tries to get the happiness which is lacking by going after objects. But, ultimately fails. My thought was one thing, but the fact is another thing. So marriage ends in divorce. 'I have no children. So I don't have happiness. All have children'. You go after children. You want children. You try to go to a doctor, consult some one and try to get blessings of a saint. And when the children come, perhaps they become the cause of great unhappiness, great anxiety, great sorrow. This is the case with every object.

There is delusion. We mistake impermanent things for permanent ones and go after them, and then when they come to an end, we are plunged in sorrow. It is like children getting delighted when you go to a fair and you get them a big balloon. They laugh, they rejoice, and after some time, when the balloon bursts, they start weeping. In the same way, the impermanent and the transitory are taken to be permanent and vainly one hopes for happiness from the impermanent. When it is suddenly destroyed, then happiness turns into misery. Because, you made a primary error, and that primary error was a perverted knowledge, wrong knowledge. Perception was not correct, was wrong knowledge. So, taking the unreal for the reality, and making one's life a complete quest for happiness, will end in unhappiness.

Pleasure Mistaken For Happiness

Delusion is also a process of the mind. And this delusion is very peculiar. Without using the intelligence, without stopping to enquire, investigate and analyse, we take for granted certain things and make it the basis of our activity, and then we find ourselves in a very pitiable situation. How? We mistake pain for pleasure. If you go deeply into an analysis of this universe, you will suddenly discover that there is not one vestige of happiness or pleasure in this universe. Not even as a mustard seed. This entire universe, this outer phenomenal world contains not one vestige of real happiness. Analysis makes this perfectly clear to you. Pleasure is one thing, and happiness or joy is totally a different thing. The human being concludes wrongly, through delusion, that pleasure is the same as happiness or joy, and tries to be happy by attaining pleasure, but finds that pleasure does not bring joy. After all, what is pleasure? Pleasure is enjoyment of senseobject through one of the five senses, and all such experience which covers the entire range of so-called human experience, will be discovered to be mere gross, physical, biological phenomenon, biological process. If you analysc all experiences of senseobjects, they are either coming into contact of the eye with an object of sight, or coming into contact of the ear with an object of sound, or coming into contact of the sense of touch with a physical object or coming into contact of tongue, the sense of taste, with an object of taste, or coming into contact of the nose with an object of smell.

These go to make up the sense-experience of the human individual in this universe. Analyse this. What is this? This coming into contact with one or another of your five senses with its respective object, is purely an animal process. It is something duplicated in the life of every animal. This coming into contact of your sense with its respective object—when it comes into contact what happens? A certain message is sent from the sensory organ of yours to that particular sensory field through one terminal of a nerve network system. When you touch an object, a tactile nerve works and that conveys from counter sensory nerve an impulse into its respective brain centre and in the brain centre a certain irritation is created, a certain stimulation is there; and you perceive that I have touched something. If that particular nerve network is not functioning, it will mean nothing to you. This irritation, this stimulation brought about in that particular brain centre is interpreted by the mind in a particular way. Why? Due to previous memory. These senses have gone through previously these sense-experiences and so, in your computer of the mind they live. When the mind says 'yes', we call it pleasure, a pleasant sensation. If the mind says 'no' and rejects it, it is a painful sensation. That is pain. So with everything. If your eyes come into contact with some shape, form or colour, light rays are reflected on the retina, and the ocular nerve, optic nerve takes it to the respective brain centre of sight and immediately that brain centre is stimulated or there is a certain irritation in the brain centre and the mind which is the feeler of all these various stimulations interprets it either positively or negatively, 'yes' or 'no', and these can change also.

If at a particular period in your life, you like something, mind always says 'yes' to it. When later on, due to some bitter experience, you saw the evil effects of that, and that which you liked one time, you began to like no longer. Then the pattern of the mind and reaction became different. That which said 'yes' formerly, now says 'no'. That which was pleasurable before, now becomes painful. You don't want it. You don't want to accept it. So, it is all a question of how your mind is conditioned, and thus the sum total of all objective experience of man, when analysed is proved to be nothing but a pure biological process of conveying of some sense-contact through a particular network of nerves to a specific centre in the brain and creating in the brain centre a certain stimulation which is purely objective depending upon some object. It cannot be joy. It cannot be a conscious subjective experience. It is not a state of mind at all. It is only a certain reaction in the mind to a certain external stimulant. And, therefore, to call it joy is a delusion. Call it pleasure and not joy. Pleasure is not happiness. Pleasure is a mere biological process. It is a gross sense-experience. But, humanity has been under this delusion so long, that it has become part of its spontaneous nature, has become natural. Take for granted that you have many objects and you possess them. If you feel you are secure and think they can make you happy, there cannot be a greater mistake. But this mistake is universal. It is taken to be correct, and man still obstinately, blindly pursues sense-experience in his quest after happiness. And the result is, it is predestined to fail.

Because, joy or happiness is at a higher level of your being. It is a state of Consciousness. It is a state of the mind. It is not a biological or a physical process. It has nothing to do with the nervous system. It has nothing to do with the brain. On the contrary, if you go deeply into an analysis you will recognise that the moment you give up this sense-urge, this continuous hunting after sense-experience, you suddenly begin to find that you have that joy, that happiness which hitherto you never had. So, the very giving up of this feverish pursuit after sense-experience becomes the condition, the prerequisite for coming into a state of contentment, joy and happiness. Even this so-called deluded concept of pleasure, if it is further expounded, if you try to analyse this experience, it will become clear to you that even this temporary sensation that is labelled pleasant for the time being, which is bringing you to a state of so-called happiness, is really no positive experience at all. It is only a temporary cessation of some type of pain.

For example, a person goes into a restaurant and has his lunch. He enjoys the lunch. He enjoys the dishes. He says it is a wonderful lunch. It gave him pleasure. But what was the actual state? What is the actual structure or anatomy of this experience he just had? He was hungry. And this hunger bothered him. It was a demand of a physical nature for food and it made him restless. Hunger was an uncomfortable experience, and as it began to grow and continued, he became restless. So, he did not want to continue it, prolong it. He could not tolerate it, and therefore he wished to put an end to this painful condition of hunger and the taking of the lunch brought about a cessation of the pain. How long? Till hunger starts once again, may be in the evening. So, the interval between two states of painful experience, when filled by a temporary stoppage of that state by some process, you label that process pleasure.

You are shivering in the cold, you get caught in the rain. Then some one invites you, takes away your coat, puts your legs in the basin of hot water, and gives you a hot cup of coffee. Now you put yourself in a warm blanket and you think you are enjoying a very comfortable state. But it is only that painful condition in which you were a moment before that has been cancelled by this, and that cessation of pain you take for positive experience. It is not positive experience at all. So those who have entered into an analysis of all sense-experience reach this discovery that what man labels as pleasure is nothing but an interval between two states of painful experience, just an intrigue interval. This is delusion. But the mind is constantly in this delusion.

And the fourth activity of the mind is, as we have just now seen, in sleep. That is also an obstacle. Because in the state of sleep, there is a total extinction of consciousness temporarily, and the Self is not realised. You are not aware of the bliss and joy of the Self. That is its defect. Otherwise, it is a perfect experience. If you try to evaluate it in terms of waking consciousness, sleep is a wonderful state, because it liberates you from everything. A beggar also attains the same state as an emperor or a multimillionaire attains. One who is poor, a beggar, nothing to eat—if he goes into deep sleep state, he is no different in experience than a multimillionaire who has gone into deep sleep state. But here, there is no awareness of the Self. It is the fourth mood or it is the fourth state the mind-activities assume.

The fifth state is the most bothersome of all. The constant perception of things is the process of knowledge; perverted knowledge is mistaking things temporary for the permanent, etc.; delusion is mistaking pain for pleasure, and thinking that if I possess things, I will be satisfied; and then sleep—these are the four activities which we have already seen.

The last activity is memory. Impressions of past experience are constantly coming into your mind. You can never overcome the past. You can never master the past. Constantly come thoughts of the past memories of previous experiences, whose impressions have already found lodged in your mind. They are constantly coming into your mind. And this is the fifth activity. All these five activities have to be overcome. You must be able to master your memory. You must be able to overcome sleep. You must be able to remove delusion. You must be able to convert perverted knowledge into right knowledge and you must be able to check and get into your control the ceaseless activity of perception and knowledge in the mind.

Why? Because, it is directed to external world, towards the many. Therefore, it becomes an obstacle to go inward and rest upon the One, wherein alone lies fullness, wherein alone lies true satisfaction, wherein alone lies true happiness, wherein alone lies true experience of Bliss, wherein alone lies the true peace and which is to be had within yourself and not outside. Therefore, to overcome these activities, we have to find out the practices.

Dispassion And Withdrawal

First of all, Patanjali gives the practice in two words briefly and then he goes on to elaborate their details. He says this overcoming can be done firstly by developing dispassion towards all things, seen or unseen, all experiences which you see before you, which you have already undergone and which you might not have experienced but you have heard about them from others. Give up completely craving, desire and thirst for all experiences, seen as well as heard.

Then you must constantly practise driving the mind, taking the mind inward, turning it away from outer sense-perception, and making it fixed upon the one inner objective. Why is this? Why did not Patanjali say merely continuous application and practice, that is the way to overcome the mind. Why did he tag into it dispassion or ceasing to thirst or desire after sense-experience? Because this is something which does not appeal to men. They ask: can we not practise Yoga and at the same time have our dancing and drinking and other pleasures also?

It is simple. If something has caught fire, you call the Fire Brigade and they are doing everything to put the fire down by pouring water. Then, when they are trying to put the fire out, logically, you cannot expect them to succeed if you are putting some petrol, oil and other things back into the fire. You have to withdraw all combustible material nearby. You must try to take them away. The fuel has to be withdrawn and you must make an attempt to extinguish the fire. If you make the attempt to extinguish the fire, and at the same time, go on supplying fresh material for burning, then you are working against yourself.

So, as you are trying to overcome the propensity of the mind sense-ward, towards pleasures, towards sense-experience, you will have to help this process by withdrawing the fuel, not go on adding to the fire of craving fresh and fresh sense-enjoyment. Because, unfortunately, the mind is such an intricate and mysterious thing, the moment you provide it with a sense-experience, immediately it makes a photographic impression of the sensation, a lightning impression of the sense-experience, and this immediate, instantaneous impression becomes the basis of a further movement towards the self-same experience, just as the grooves that are in a gramophone record or an invisible impression created in a tape. Every sound that has been put into it has the power and the capacity to recreate the same sound at given condition. In the same way, every impression that finds enlodgement within the mind has the power, just as a seed has a power to recreate the entire tree out of itself. These impressions are not merely inert or static.

They are alive. They are dynamic. They create in the mind a tendency towards the selfsame experience. Therein lies the need to be careful regarding them. If you go on continuing sense-experience, you go on putting new impressions and the mind will always be in a state of sense-oriented activity. Because, these impressions are constantly being freshly put in. So, while you are trying to annihilate the experience already created, you have to simultaneously put a stop for the inflow of fresh experiences, fresh impressions which are called 'Samskaras' in Sanskrit.

So, this putting a stop to fresh experiences and impressions is called Vairagya or turning away from a passionate longing for sense-experience, a craving for sense-experience, a thirsting after sense experience, and it is called dispassion. So, simultaneously, there should be an effort and practice to concentrate, turn the mind inward, at the same time, withdraw the senses from the sense-objects, withdraw the mind from the senses and withdraw yourself even from the mind. There should be then three-way (triple) withdrawal. As far as possible, let not the senses go towards the sense-objects.

Secondly, even if the senses are amidst sense-objects, let not the mind go towards sense-objects in order to enjoy it or experience it. And even if sometimes, the mind through force of habit goes, you separate from it and say: "No, now I am in quest of something greater, something infinitely grand. So I will not go for the passing petty. I will not go for the little. I want that which is complete, the whole and that will give me eternal satisfaction. Therefore, I refuse to link myself with the mind and move towards the senses and go towards the objects." You withdraw yourself from the mind and the senses.

In this way, Patanjali formulates a ceaseless turning away from desire, turning away from sense-objects and sense-experience. A ceaseless pursuit of practice with regularity, with persistence and with intensity is required. The means employed also should be intense. In this way, if you persist in this practice continuously, with keen interest, you will attain success.

You have to be interested in yourself. I cannot be interested and give you highest welfare. Someone else cannot be interested to give you highest joy. You have to be interested in yourself. Therefore, with keen interest, you persist in this effort and continuously carry on over a long period of time. Success is certain. That is the declaration of Yoga in and through Patanjali's Yoga Sutras.

Today, in as much as last night, I conclude my talk. We will take up the different means suggested for succeeding in the attempt to overcome the mental activities in the form of right knowledge through perception, wrong knowledge or perverted knowledge, delusion about the real state of things, sleep and memory. In what way one can succeed through different practices, and one can attain a peaceful and serene state of mind? That we will take up next time.

Third Lecture:
Mind and its Activity

Radiant Immortal Atman! Beloved seekers after the Divine! To refresh your memories, I shall just very briefly sum up in a very few sentences the ground covered last Monday. Continuing from the very first talk on Friday, the 13th April, we considered initially, the very basic nature of the mind-principle which was seen to be outgoing in its nature. We later observed that how this outward movement of the mind-stuff was responsible for man's involvement in matter, soul's involvement, enmeshing itself in fluctuating and unstable, universal process which we call the world.

After this, we saw how this involvement is phenomenal in the changeful, the passing and the perishable. This involvement has alienated the pure Consciousness from its original centre, or in other words from its pristine state of experience of peace and joy. We also saw how all human experience is due to this activity which on one side involved you in the phenomenon and simultaneously deprived you of self-experience. This mental activity was seen to be the very basic of all human experiences. We try to bring home, this central fact of philosophy, by drawing attention to the universally observed experience of the human being, each day, day after day, throughout life, namely, the disappearance of the world, disappearance of all things seen, with the cessation of mind-activity every night when you enter into deep sleep. So, this is a universally uncontradicted experience of human beings throughout their life.

But the deep significance of it has never been pondered. No one paid attention to it. No one pays attention to the sun. He rises every morning. One of the grandest, beautiful and sublime things, but no one has got an eye for it. Taking for granted, in the same way, this vital experience brings you this startling truth that the world-experience is no other than mental activity. It has no other basis than mental activity. If there is mental activity, world is before you. The moment mental activity ceases completely, world also disappears, your own body disappears, your identity also disappears. When you are in deep sleep, you don't know whether you are a human being or an animal, male or female, old or young, rich or poor, learned or ignorant, Occidental or Oriental. All awareness of one's own being in the relative sense of the term, is totally merged and drowned. The universe and yourself both disappear and you experience this annihilation of yourself and recognition. Simultaneously, you also experience that from that moment of your emerging into waking state, some faculty of your mind restarting again its activities, and from that moment the reality of the world stands before you. You also attain once again your self-awareness. So, with the mind, the world and your ego-consciousness rise and set. When the mind sinks in the oblivion of sleep, your own ego-consciousness also sinks and sets and the world also sinks.

And with the rising again of mental activity once again, the world emerges before you, stands before you. You perceive it. You are also aware of yourself. So, this very significant personality of being was pondered. Universal experience of all human beings throughout life vividly brings out before us the fact that the basis of all human experience, all phenomenal perceptions, is mental activity. And therefore, involvement in this experience, in this phenomenal perception, being the factors that deprived you of Self-realisation or Self-awareness, naturally mind-activity seems to be the basis of your involvement. In that basis of your involvement, or in other words, in the basis of your Samsara is the root-cause for the non-perception of the Self within. This activity manifests itself in the form of various perceptual processes; and the subdual of these perceptual processes was, therefore, defined as Yoga.

Chittavritti (mental modifications) manifests itself in the form of waves of perceptive processes. In our previous class, we saw how these perceptual processes take various forms. Every moment, we are gaining this knowledge, direct knowledge by seeing through the eyes, by smelling through the nose, by hearing through the ears, by tasting through the tongue and by touching through the hands. So in this way, we keep on gathering knowledge of the universe around us, direct knowledge through senseperception.

Secondly, we have perverted, wrong perception also. What the eye sees is not always correct. We receive wrongly-perverted knowledge. Perverted knowledge is mistaking one thing for another thing, mistaking pleasure for happiness, mistaking the very source of pain, i.e., sense-objects which constantly keep the mind in agitation. We think, we will find pleasure in them. We think we will find happiness in them. So, our idea is that if we obtain things and possess them and experience them, we will be happy. Because, we don't have things, we do not possess them and we cannot experience them, we are unhappy. This is the peculiar idea of the mind, wrong emotion of the mind. In the Bhagavad-Gita, the entire range of such experiences brought about by a particular sense-organ coming into contact with its respective sense-object, is depicted beautifully. All such experiences brought about by contact of the senses with sense-objects were characterised by Lord Krishna, the great teacher of Gita, as the source of pain.

"O Arjuna, all these experiences, pleasurable experiences brought about by the contact of the senses with their respective sense-objects—these experiences are the sources of pain. The wise do not take delight in such pleasurable experiences. Because, they know that in the beginning they give a little satisfaction, later on they bring about pain, they bring about sorrow, bring about misery. Therefore, the wise shun them. They recognise such experiences to be ultimately the cause of pain, sorrow and suffering. Therefore, they do not take delight in it." Thus, Krishna characterised all pleasurable experiences brought about by contacting sense-objects as pain, not pleasure.

But yet, by and large, the vast majority of human beings have the idea that we shall be happy if we manage to obtain objects of our desire. So, this is perverted knowledge, contradicting all human experience. But man refuses to learn. Mind will not allow him to learn. Again and again, he is disillusioned and he thinks: "May be next time, I will obtain happiness." Even when it is painful, he says always 'next time', and the Guru of Swami Vivekananda, the great sage of Dakshinesvar, Sri Ramakrishna has described this in a quaint village analogy.

The Parable Of A Camel

Even now, in certain parts of India, where the climate is not so cold, camels are used as draft animals. They draw carts, take loads and transport goods. May be not so prevalent as in Arabia, but still it is there. Observing their habits, Sri Ramakrishna said: "Such is the nature of the vast majority of human beings; again and again, they go towards senseobjects, expecting happiness and joy from them. Instead of happiness and joy, they only get pain and suffering. But still, such is the nature of man that in spite of being disillusioned again and again, he goes towards these objects." And, he described:

"In deserts these camels go and nibble thorny plants (in most of the deserts, the plants are thorny) and thorns prick their lips and even injure them, and they even cause bleeding but yet the camels do not leave these plants. Though bleeding, they still persist in eating these plants." He says such is the nature of man. He gets suffering when he runs after perishable objects and yet he will persist in going after these. It is perverted knowledge. Delusion is taking appearances for reality, being unable to perceive reality behind appearances due to lack of discrimination, lack of proper enquiry. This is another mood in which the mind is constantly operating, expressing itself active.

The State Of Sleep

The fourth is sleep state. That is also a mood of the mind. It is a Vritti. When you are tired from all this continuous process of perceiving the world, coming into contact with it, moving with people, reacting to environment and situation, when you are tired, then a time comes when the mind does not want it and the mind wants to go into a state which is characterised by the absence of these perceptions. So, when there is in the mind the desire to be free from mental processes, it is said that the mind catches on to a desire or thought of nothing. So, this Vritti is the spontaneous, innate desire of the mind to hold on to nothingness, hold on to a thoughtless state. When the desire comes, the tired personality wants to sleep.

Memory

The fifth mood with which the mind operates, is the activity of the mind which expresses itself, manifests itself as your knowing in the form of memory, all past things inside. Specially, the memory troubles a great deal either when you are alone or not engaged, not actively occupied. When your mind is not directed and is doing nothing, then what happens is, you brood over the past. The past things start coming into the mind and they cause distraction. You have all heard the expression 'wool-gathering', and especially is this mentioned here. Quite apart from the universal habit of woolgathering or brooding over the past, it is very very bad with you, because, it creates various moods in the mind. If you have been hurt by people or things, then resentment comes, or it takes you over things which have been painful to you, which have been sorrowful—partings, deaths, bereavements, failures—then you go into a sorrowful state. Even otherwise, you go into a state of dejection, when the mind dwells upon all that you desired but could not obtain. Your failures, your frustrations make your mind dejected. So, various mental moods are thrown up by unnecessary and avoidable memory.

Therefore, the masters always instruct or advise spiritual seekers never to be without some occupation. Therefore, keep yourself engaged. If you cannot meditate or study or worship, then do some physical exercise, gardening, service to the poor and the sick. Some sort of occupation should always be there. Mind should never be without occupation or activity. Otherwise, it falls back into unnecessary dwelling upon the past and then have all its negative reactions upon the mind. The specific period when memory becomes a most troublesome activity of the mind is, when you want to meditate, when you close the avenue of senses and sit at one place. Don't go here and there, close your eyes and fix your mind on the object of your concentration. There is no distraction from the outer world because you have closed yourself from the outer world. But then, the submerged impressions of the previous experiences in the form of memory work great havoc in the mind. These are the five moods that Vrittis express themselves. That is, mind-modifications actively fill the mind and these, therefore, are the different moods and activities of the mind which you have to tackle, which you have to deal with. You have to try to bring it into your control, subdue and master. So, it is very much the area in which the student of Raja Yoga is concerned. For over coming these little modifications, success in concentration is very essential; and the means suggested by Patanjali Maharshi are twofold. Here, we have a very interesting, noteworthy parallel to the Gita. Identical words are used and they are 'Abhyasa' and 'Vairagya' (practice and dispassion).

Abhyasa And Vairagya (Practice And Dispassion)

In our previous lecture, we concluded briefly upon practice and dispassion. Practice, you all can understand. Nothing comes unless we practise. While in the process of subduing and effacing the mind-impressions which have already been gathered, if you are constantly running after sense-pleasures and putting into the mind more and more impressions, then it will be a never-ending process. Here you are trying to wipe them out, keeping up the perennial supply of new impressions to your mind. I gave you the analogy of how to put out a fire—while you are trying to put the fire out, at the same time you will have to withdraw the fuel. Instead of that, while you try to put out the fire, if you go on putting more combustible materials into the fire, then you are fighting against yourself. You will not be able to succeed in it. In the same way, if you want to put out the blaze of the constant mental activity and various modifications, while you are engaged in doing it, you must also wisely see that you don't add fresh fuel to this mental activity. So, the need to support the practice by self-control, dispassion (nonattachment), turning away from cravings for the passing things. This is a twofold inseparable Sadhana, Vairagya and Abhyasa (non-attachment or dispassion and constant practice).

Patanjali has a word to say about how practice shall be, if it should be successful. The practice should be over a long period of time, carried on continuously in an unbroken way, with keen interest in it. You must evince keen interest. You should not do Sadhana (practice) by fits. You start vigorous Sadhana for a few weeks, but afterwards something happens; for two or three days no Sadhana, you could not do anything and then you give it up for two or three months, then nothing. Then, you read some magazine or listen to some inspired talk; again take up, barely for some time. This kind of Sadhana is no good. Even if you do little, do it continuously, without break. Unfailing regularity is important. Patanjali Yoga Sutras say that practice becomes steady and successful, if it is over a long period of time, continuously. The practice should be unbroken and carried on for a long period of time. You should have a keen interest and your Sadhana should be supported by Vairagya (dispassion). Then alone you will attain success.

This was a method also suggested by Lord Krishna in the Gita, when He instructed Arjuna, on the process of Yoga, in the sixth chapter. After listening to the Sadhana or spiritual practice outlined by Lord Krishna, Arjuna says: "It is very nice for you to describe it, but I think it is of no use to me, because I believe that the mind is so absolutely uncontrollable, so completely full of Rajas that one may very well be able to control the wind, the waves of the sea, but not the mind. It is impossible. So, what is the use of describing Yoga to me!" When Arjuna responds in this way, in a very negative way to Lord Krishna's description of Yoga, Krishna gives a very significant reply. He does not contradict Arjuna. He doesn't say mind is very easy to control.

We have many teachers who say this. They may be shrewd psychologists, I admit. May be, they don't want to frighten people, likely seekers, saying that the mind is very, very difficult to control, right from the beginning. So, if you say it is very easy, at least man starts. But overdoing this also is unfair. Because, with much eagerness and with much expectation, some of the seekers will come, they will do the techniques for some time, after some time they get spectacular effect to some extent, and afterwards there they get stuck. Nothing further comes out of it. They lose all faith. They will never afterwards take it up. They will say: "We have only been duped, nothing can come out of it." So, *via media is* better. Be realistic. The mind is very difficult to control. It is not an easy joke. At the same time, it is possible if you regularly practise. Don't be discouraged. It is possible. Many have succeeded. Go on practising without giving it up. And one day you will reach the Goal. In this way, it is better not to conceal the fact. But do not give frightening exaggeration. If you hear the statements of some masters of Yoga in India about the mind, you will never practise Yoga. You will give it up.

It is easier to drink the ocean in the palm of your hand, it is easier to fly in the air, it is easier to pierce a diamond with a filament of a flower, it is easy to catch hold and restrain a mad elephant with a spider's web it is easier to make the fire burn downward, it is easier to catch hold of a lion or a tiger and milk it, but it is not easy to control the mind. All these can be done. But it is not an easy task to bring the mind under your control. Such are the ways or words in which they describe the super-human task of controlling the mind, but yet at the same time, they never said it is impossible— precisely as the great Master Krishna says. He agrees with Arjuna: "Yes, Arjuna! You are right. Difficult it is to control the mind. I agree, but you are wrong when you say that it is impossible to control the mind. I firmly assure you, and emphatically declare that it is possible for you to control the mind." And uses precisely the same words of Patanjali.

The Different Grades Of Concentration

He says: 'By regular practice and through dispassion.' How practice has to be? How dispassion has to be? It should be based upon discrimination, not merely an emotional upsurge, not merely a sentiment. By hearing some fiery sermon, immediately you conceive dispassion—'No, I will give up everything, I will shave off my hair.' You go to extremes, just upon an emotional upsurge. Seeing the cinema of the life of St. Francis of Assisi or some other saint, immediately next day, you start wanting to give up everything. Extremes should not be done. All extremes should be avoided. Dispassion becomes the outcome of reflecting upon the real nature of the world or enquiring the real nature of things and by association with the seekers and Sadhakas, and your own gradual understanding. Then, that dispassion becomes real. Now, the result of such concentration will ultimately be the study of the mind, having known its nature, having known the connection between world-experience and mental activity. Thus understanding the basis of Yoga, launch yourself upon the practice with dispassion and continued practice and concentration in the mind, subduing all the mental activities. If through such application, you succeed in attaining progressive states of concentration, what happens to you. What all the different states of concentration you reach? And what is the consequence of it? What experience you gain?—become the subject of Patanjali.

In the next few Sutras Patanjali says that these states of inner concentration which the seeker obtains are supported by dispassion, when he carries on his practice vigorously with keen interest.

The states are classified into varieties and he commences by giving us the description of one variety of this intense inner concentration, a state which he characterises or terms as Samadhi—trance. And one kind of this type of intense, inner concentration, trance, is what is known as the Cognitive Trance. It is by concentrating on one object, cognising one object and concentrating upon it, various inner experiences are brought about. You reach various states of inner concentration. One state is when you concentrate upon the object as it appears to you. So it can be upon any object. You concentrate inwards, a consideration as the object presents itself to your mind through the different senses. For instance, the table, I can see it, at the same time I can touch it. Two senses are involved in my perception of a table. More than two senses also can be involved, three or four senses also can be involved. When a person eats a thing, it comes into contact with the lips, tongue and palate. So there is a contact and at the same time, you taste it and the aroma of it also is experienced. In this way, as an object presents itself to your mind, you concentrate upon it and gain an intense state of unified thought focused upon that object. All other thoughts are kept away. So, you get absorbed in the focusing and that intense state of absorption in concentrating upon an object as it presents itself to you, is the first state where you try to gain knowledge of all aspects of that thing. What it is to you? How it presents itself? How it appears to you? So, it is accompanied by a philosophical enquiry, or an examination of that object from all angles, from all aspects.

Then, this same concentration can now switch on into another dimension. Start focusing upon the inner implications of that object, the very essence of the object, instead of the object as it presents itself to you to the senses, the object as you are understanding. You go deeper into the very essence, the very nature of the object. What it is useful for? How it came into being? What is its place in the universe, in what way you are related to it and in what way it is related to you—concentration on an object in depth, the subtler and inner aspect of it, the essence of the thing, not in its appearance. Here, there is discrimination between the outer appearance of the object and the subtle inner nature of the object. This concentration, this state is accompanied by discrimination, Vichara. Vichara is subtler and inner. It is more meditative in its nature.

Thirdly, the concentration which you thus carry on, may move now from the object to the very process of perceiving and concentrating upon the object. So, now the concentration actually moves into the area of the mind itself. Who is doing this perception? Who is doing this focusing? Who is doing this concentration or examination of the object? The mind. So, this mind-process, perceptual process of the mind, becomes now the object of your concentration. And as you were absorbed in the object, you now begin to focus the attention upon the process of being focused upon the object, upon the process of being absorbed in the object. So the mental process becomes the object of your concentration. More subtle, more inward, and gradually turning towards the subject, in its depth. Concentration is much deeper and your being is freed from the bondage of the object. Now, this concentration frees you from the impact of the object or your reaction to it, your feelings towards it. Therefore, this sense of being forced from the objective world to the Cognitive Perception gives you a sense of elation, a sense of joy. Every kind of freedom, every step you move towards a liberated state, is always characterised by enhanced joy. So, in this state of concentration where the mind is taken away from the shackles of an object for its support and moves into the area of activity itself, the object of attention, it is accompanied by a subtler feeling of joy. This concentration is accompanied not by examination of the details of an object, not even by an entering into discrimination or enquiry into the real nature of an object, but by a feeling of joy.

The fourth form of the intense inner concentration takes you inward from even the observation of the mental perception, and focuses your attention on yourself, as distinct from the mental perceptional process, from the inner essence of the object to which it was directed to, and even from the appearance of the object itself. So, the object is given up and even the essential nature, subtle nature of the object is given up and even the concentration or focusing yourself upon the perceptual process is given up. You focus your attention merely upon you who are the seer of those things, you who are the subject, who are carrying on this process. You remain aware as the subject, as distinct from even the perceptual process and the object originally concentrated upon. Here, it is the innermost state, you are aware of yourself only as the seeing subject, the meditator, but then this 'I' upon which the mind is now focused, is not yet the universal Consciousness. It is not the pure Consciousness. Yet it is the individualised consciousness. These are the four ways or the four aspects which concentration upon an object can take. Intensified state of consciousness is a distinct progress in the practice of Yoga. It is a great deal of progress in concentration. It is successful concentration.

Now apart from this, there is another state of deep, intense concentration inward, where no object is your focal point. The focal point is entirely inside. The mind is completely tuned within and there is an absence of any object in the focal point of your attention and thought-flow. The mind contact in its inner submerged state, that alone is there in the field of your attention. That is the Chitta, the subconscious. The various Samskaras alone remain. There is no outer object as a focal point, but only the inner content of the mind. This is much more subtle, much more inner. When the mind is absorbed into itself, it is called the higher process. The other state of concentration is far more subtler, inward and subjective and has nothing as its objective, rather has the inner mind content only, by keeping out all objective thoughts through the checking of thought-waves by continuous non-attachment or dispassion in the true spiritual aspirant. How this inner state of intense concentration is achieved? How does one achieve progress in two types of concentration upon an object, in its four aspects, and concentration upon no object but upon the mind, upon the inner content of the mind itself? By faith.

Faith Brings Progress

First of all, the aspirant must have intense faith in the Yoga he practises and the goal to which he is moving, and in the validity of the process which he is adapting. Faith grows and develops by associating with similar seekers. If we associate with people of other types, hedonists, materialists, people who have no faith in the higher life or anything, whatever little faith you have, you would lose it. Therefore, you must carefully protect this spiritual Samskara. It becomes necessary to avoid the company of those who scoff at these things or make fun of these things. For, they have no belief in these. Therefore, the spiritual aspirant has to be selective. He should mix only with seekers. A spiritual aspirant has to be selective in choosing his company. He must try to move among such company who have similar ideal and aspiration, who are also moving towards the selfsame experience, believing in the goal which he believes in and who have faith in the higher values of life. The more faith you have, the greater energy you get in your pursuit and your practice is backed up by energy. If you want to do vigorous practice, then have intense faith. The degree of faith decides the intensity of your practice.

You must read books which bring out the experiences of other seekers who have trodden the path, covered this area and attained the goal. And this testimony increases your faith. Company of holy people, meeting saints actually, reading the lives of saints, Yogic Masters who have trodden the path and attained illumination. There you find the sublime character of their personal life and their experiences. At the same time, if you can get the opportunity of coming into direct contact with people who are rooted in that experience, that is of course, the best of all things. The company of seekers of your own sort and your energetic practices with faith will gradually bring about certain stability in your mind. Gradually the dissipated and distracted mind which was scattered among multifarious things, begins to get ingathered. So, gradually the mind now gets the tendency of not wanting to get distracted, it would give attention only to things which are necessary and not to unnecessary things.

Miscellaneous thoughts now gradually become distasteful to the mind. So the mind gets collected. It is called recollectedness. When you reach the state of recollectedness of the mind, naturally the tendency of the mind becomes more and more absorbed in the object of concentration. It becomes spontaneous inclination of the mind to get absorbed and through this absorption you attain illumination. So, success in concentration in the true spiritual aspirant comes as a result of faith. The energy gained through such faith, the recollectedness results from such energetic practice and the absorption to which one is led by such recollectedness, takes one ultimately to illumination.

These then are the factors that go to bring about successful concentration in a true spiritual aspirant. Sage Patanjali uses the words 'true spiritual aspirant', because people may approach Yoga ostensibly for realisation, but their real quest may be for the wonderful powers that are described in the books on Yoga. You can do this, you can do that. Many people attracted by these great powers, may take to the practice of Yoga and get the powers, but they will not get illumination. So, Patanjali makes a distinction between people who take to Yoga for lesser ends and the true spiritual aspirant who is the seeker after God-experience or Illumination. In him, naturally, there will be all these five factors. Faith is the bliss. Faith, energy, recollectedness, absorption—all these factors lead to Illumination.

Now, Patanjali brings us to a consideration of some very practical things. When one launches forth into such seeking, in spite of all equipments such as sincerity, earnestness and all that, obstacles come on the way to progress. Obstacles are numerous. They may differ from person to person. But some of the general obstacles are likely to come to most persons. Because, they are common to man as an embodied being with a mind and its mischief. He lists a certain number of obstacles and gives us very practical methods of dealing with them successfully and overcoming them. The basic obstacle is sickness. Sickness comes through lack of self-control and self-control can come only by discipline.

The Importance Of Hatha Yoga

If there is no discipline in life, one cannot have self-control and it is in this connection that Hatha Yoga becomes very relevant, of very great importance to all people who wish to enter into the inner Yoga, Raja Yoga and meditation. Hatha Yoga has a direct effect in giving you an increased state of health. It is because of these reasons that Hatha Yoga gained much importance. As you know, each particular Asana in Hatha Yoga has an effect on some particular part of your inner machinery, inner mechanism. Some have beneficial effect on the heart. Some have beneficial effect on the lungs, beneficial effect on the brain, beneficial effect on the nervous system and some have beneficial effect upon the autonomous nervous system kept along the spinal column. Some have beneficial effect upon liver, spleen and pancreas. In this way, the respiratory system, the circulatory system, the digestive system, etc., stand to gain positive, immediate and direct benefit by different Asanas of Hatha Yoga. So, real health comes due to a regular practice of Hatha Yoga in the spiritual path. Secondly, Hatha Yogic exercises like Asanas, Mudras, Bandhas, have a special connection with relation to the three Gunas in the human system, physical and mental.

So, Hatha Yoga has the unfailing effect as no other system of psycho-physical culture in the world has. It has the unfailing effect of gradually eliminating Tamas from the human system, human nature, and effectively controlling, giving you control over the Rajas and increasing Sattva. There is no known means of increasing Sattva and eliminating Tamas as effective as Hatha Yoga. Of course diet-control, Sattvic diet, keeping company with Sattvic people, no doubt, will bring you certain amount of Sattva but Hatha Yoga is an effective unfailing technique. It is scientific. Hatha Yoga helps you gradually putting Tamas under your control and increasing Sattva steadily and progressively, and through this comes self-control. It is a marvel. It is a state of discipline.

Hatha Yoga is the system of discipline or training. If the senses are not coming under your control, if they are turbulent, uncontrollable, then you put yourself through a period of Hatha Yogic training, you will begin to find that you are able to control the senses.

Obstacles In The Path Of Yoga

What is the secret? The senses are turbulent because of too much of Rajo Guna, and you are unable to control because you are too much Tamasic. Tamas makes your will weak. You cannot control it. If Sattva increases will power increases. Simultaneously, when Rajo-Guna also is subdued then you are able to control the senses.

So, here sickness can be overcome by Hatha Yoga. Moderation in diet, regularity in habits, eating, drinking, sleeping, going to bed, regularity of life, all these will help you to overcome sickness.

Then indolence is another obstacle. Mental indolence, postponing habits, unwillingness to do things immediately when it is to be done—all these obstacles hamper one's progress in the path of Yoga.

In this context, we have to warn all young people of this age, this unfortunate generation, that one of the greatest dangers is getting addicted. All drugs will completely bring about a breakdown in the vigour of the mind and the will-power. Any narcotic has a befiddling effect on the mind and makes one lazy. The will to do a thing immediately goes away. One becomes indifferent. That is the great danger of all the narcotics that befiddle the alertness of the mind, not knowing the connection between will and drugs. You see vast majority of unfortunate young people of this generation are putting themselves to a position of danger which will retard evolution in every way, under any direction.

Vigorous habits are to be trained. These obstacles have to be overcome. Indolence and half-heartedness have to be overcome by faith. You do meditation for little time, some technique you practise, afterwards you reach a state of mindlessness, or you begin to feel some sort of an inner silence. You think, 'I have attained Samadhi,' and then, afterwards you don't want to listen to anyone at all. This is a wrong notion. Already you think that you have attained something, but you are nowhere near it. This false notion is a very terrible obstacle in the path of Sadhana. Despair by failure to succeed in concentration, is another obstacle. You go on trying and you don't succeed; and afterwards what happens is that you become hopeless and think that in this life you will not succeed. This is a very great obstacle.

These are all things which bring about a state of dejection. How to overcome these? You may have all these obstacles. You may have one, or you may have some. How to overcome them? There is only one way. You must understand here, all these obstacles are put up before you by the mind. Indolence, despair, half-heartedness, dejection— they are all moods of the mind, the mind again playing its game. Therefore, you must be alert. You have understood that entire world-experience is based upon mind-activity. Even all these obstacles now put into your way—they are also parts of the mind only. Therefore, there is only one way of overcoming them. Take up some particular object and stick to it with leach-like tenacity and don't give it up. It may bring about dejection, hopelessness and procrastination. Don't listen to it. Be at it vigorously, stick to one thing. Stick to it with leach-like tenacity and go on practising: Come what may 'Men may come and men may go but I go on for ever'—in this way, stick to it. Don't leave it. This is called Ekatattva Abhyasa—taking up one thing and sticking to it like a leech.

Secondly, transform mental attitudes. These various things are brought about by our association in this world. Many a time, mind is upset and perturbed by our association with people and our daily dealing with people and our environment. Have a transformed attitude. Keep the mind always pleased. Keep the mind always calm and always peaceful. This is the secret of overcoming obstacles of the mind. Patanjali says: 'Be always cheerful'.

How To Overcome Obstacles

Don't be dejected yourself. Whenever you see anyone happy you also rejoice. Be joyful at the happiness of others. And be moved with sympathy and compassion at the pain and suffering of others. Be elated when you see goodness and virtue in others, instead of being upset. 'What a wonderful person he is! I will also be able to attain that state.' See when you compare with someone very very good, very very noble, you feel how unworthy you are. This is another way of overcoming the obstacles and having a fresh vigour and interest in your Sadhana.

Trataka is gazing upon a candle-flame or gazing upon a spot. This is one type of concentration which very easily brings you some spiritual experience within a short time, even after a month of concentration you begin to see lights. You gaze at it for some time, afterwards you would be able to visualise it in the sky, much expanded in form. Or, close your eyes and you can see it even with closed eyes. In this way, it suddenly thrills you with the ability to do things which you never thought you are capable of doing, something unusual, something novel, and this is also an encouragement.

Suppose you are concentrating on the tip of the nose. If your concentration is very regular, what will happen within a short time, in a couple of months? You begin to smell some wonderful fragrance. So, there are some special types of concentration which bring about immediate result and this novel experience becomes a food to the aspirant. It is very encouraging. You may also meditate upon inner lights. Feel that the Light of lights, the supreme light of God, the ray of Divine Light is here in this heart-shrine, and meditation upon that Light becomes a very elevating process. Or, you may take for your object of meditation, some illumined master, great saints, souls who have already reached perfection. Meditating upon them inspires you. It gives you great uplift in the heart and also some progress comes. You become filled with keen sense of elation and you want to become like them.

The fourth very important result of this meditation is, the more you meditate upon these ideal beings, some of their qualities begin to flow into your nature. It may be the form of a deity; it may the form of some great saint. You can also meditate upon the dream or sleep experience. If you meditate upon your being, gradually you will see the dream-like nature of the outer world. Outer world ceases to trouble you. As you meditate upon the dream and sleep states, you begin to find out why I call this dream state and sleep state as false and unreal. Why? Just because upon waking up, they become contradicted. Therefore, I say, they are not real. But is it not the same about the waking state? When I am in the dream state or in the state of deep sleep, the waking universe is not, and experiences are contradicted. So, the mere basis of one state being contradicted by another state is sufficient to dub it as unreal and false, why not apply the same rule to the other states also? The moment you go to sleep, the waking state is contradicted. When I am in dream state, the waking state is contradicted. So, why should I not say that the waking state is false, is unreal? Be fair. Apply the same criterion, the same standard for both. If you say that the waking state is real and the other two states unreal, the waking state disappears in the other two states, and I therefore say that the waking state is also unreal. Because, when I go into deep sleep state, the waking and dream states disappear: Why this double standards?

In this way, meditating upon sleep and dream states gradually frees you from the bondage of waking state experience of names and forms. And many of the obstacles based upon the outer waking world—those obstacles are to be overcome. Patanjali is so universal, that he says, ultimately, you may successfully meditate upon any object or any form which is very pleasing to you and which attracts the mind spontaneously. The mind is willing and happy to fix it upon itself. These are the various ways to overcome the obstacles and achieve a state of intense inward concentration. I close by mentioning one more very important thing.

Patanjali says that by devotion to God, all the obstacles to concentration can be overcome. And also, one can succeed in attaining inner concentration, by devotion to God. And who is that God? Patanjali says, He is the Supreme Being, who is beyond the bondage of the world-processes, who is characterised by Wisdom and Knowledge, who has no ignorance, no imperfection in Him. He is not bound by any law and is the allperfect Being, infinite in His Wisdom and the Original Master of all masters, the great Universal Master beyond all masters. If you have devotion to Him, you will succeed in Yoga. How to express and practise that devotion to Him? It is by taking His Name and simultaneously meditating upon the meaning of the Name, or anything that pleases your mind most.

Om is the symbol. So, here Patanjali does not concern himself with any of those various aspects of Hindu Pantheon. He does not say Rama, Siva, Brahma or Vishnu or any other name. He takes the Universal Being, the Almighty. His Name is one, and the repetition of Divine sound-symbol 'OM' with meditation simultaneously upon its meaning or thinking upon its meaning, is one of the unfailing methods of overcoming all obstacles and attaining success in concentration and Superconsciousness—meditation and Samadhi. This is today's talk.

Fourth Lecture:

Right Application in Yoga brings Success

Glorious Immortal Atman! Blessed children of Light! Seekers upon the path to perfection! Greetings to you all for today's fellowship. Very briefly we shall go over the main points of yesterday's talk and its preceding consideration, and then continue the subject.

At the very first talk, at the very outset, we touched upon the study of the Yoga philosophy regarding the nature of the mind and its successful control. It is the mind that draws the consciousness outside through the senses and gets involved in the appearance of the changeful world-process, names and forms. And we also saw how it was the mind's activity that was the basis or the root-cause of the entire gamut of human experiences. Within this world-process, whatever we experience is totally the product of our mind-activity. We try to understand this by a consideration of the daily experience of every human being, in each cycle of 24 hours, when he passes through the distinct states of consciousness, the waking consciousness, the dream consciousness and the sleep consciousness. We saw how sleep consciousness again and again brings home to us the fact that with the cessation of the mind-activity, experience of the worldprocess disappears, experience of even our own existence disappears. With the recommencement of mind-activity in the morning upon waking once again, our consciousness of our individual being once again rises up and with it our experience of the world-process once again begins. We saw how it was important to ponder this psychic experience of every human individual, upon which observation was based this thesis that the world-process and the experience by the individual, cannot be considered apart from his mind-activity. Upon this thesis, Patanjali formulated science by which the transcending of the mind-activity becomes the method or the means of attaining the pristine state—Self-realisation or pure Consciousness of Being. Yoga Sutras have described this in its fivefold moods of mind-activities, viz, perception, perversion, delusion, sleep and memory.

And we briefly touched upon Vairagya and Abhyasa. Yesterday, we considered the necessity of both being simultaneous and interdependent. One without the other, will not be giving us the desired result and we also answered the question, how success can be attained in this ceaseless effort. Sage Patanjali has said: 'Success comes to one who makes efforts energetically.' The success varies according to the means adopted, whether it is a mild practice, medium practice or intense practice. Intense practice will bring the highest success, medium practice will bring little success and if your practice is mild, then success may not come for a long time and it may not be the fullest kind of success. So, he has given two Sutras to answer the question. How can one succeed? Upon what does success depend in a true aspirant, or a true spiritual seeker? Because, you must never forget that Yoga is a science that aims at giving to the practitioner Divine experience. If you are approaching Yoga seeking Divine experience as your ultimate goal, then that is the classical approach and your Yoga will be authentic; but if that Divine experience is not your confirmed goal, then your Yoga might give you other experiences, other results. But then, you will still be shifting yourself from or closing yourself to the true goal and ultimate objective of Yoga in its classical sense.

Success comes to the true spiritual aspirant who has Divine experience as the ultimate goal, first and foremost, through faith that there exists that transcendental experience, there is a fulfilment of all life. There does exist an unwavering faith in the existence of that ultimate experience which is the goal. The greater the degree of faith, the more he is released into an unwavering and intense practice. Where there is doubt, the practice would be woolgathering. There is always wavering in one who knows that he is going to a wild-goose chase. 'Really is there anything to obtain?' 'Am I making a great mistake?' If there are these doubts, then the entire energy, all power that is released in the effort, will be dispersed by wavering and hesitation. I practise Yoga, may be, but, I also keep some other little objective in the world. If I don't get at the final goal, at least I will have the latter. This should not be the attitude. With a high degree of true faith, there comes greater energy in the practice; and when one practises energetically with firm faith, the entire personality potency of the being comes ingathered, collected and centralised. There is recollectedness. There is lesser room for the possibility of dispersal of one's energy in the practice. One's personality is not scattered. All faculties become centered to this one effort, this one goal. And with ingatheredness brought about by faith and energy more and more, comes deeper and deeper absorption, and this leads to illumination. In this way if the aspirant proceeds, then he gradually begins to reach a deep state of concentration where he is totally absorbed within.

Different states of the concentration are listed as the stages where one is absorbed upon an object. First is concentrating upon the object as it presents itself through one's consciousness. In the second stage, one goes beyond the mere appearance of the object goes deeper into the consideration of the very essence of the object. Then one goes beyond the name and form of the object and the whole concentration goes upon the perceptual process of the mind itself. Concentration shifts from the object to the area of the mind. Ultimately, even this is left behind and concentration becomes involved in the subject who is doing these processes. So, one concentrates upon the mere fact of one's being. That is awareness of oneself. These are the four stages of the one aspect of absorption. In the second stage there is no object at all. So the external world is no longer the field of focus of the mind of the yogi, but the internal world, that which is groundwork of dreams is in focus. So, the concentration takes place only upon the submerged impressions of previous experiences. This is a very subtle state of concentration. This is the second type of inner state of concentration, the same concentration but without object. Another means to succeed in such concentration, was also mentioned here. This shows how Yoga is very much involved in religions. Yoga, though it transcends any specific religion, is the most universal and in the basic sense of the term, Yoga is very much involved in religion. It concerns itself with the spirit of true religion. What is that spirit of universal religion? Individuals journey back into the universal. It is the quest of the human towards the Divine, or the finite moving towards its merger into Infinite, man to God. This is the essence of all religions. The universal essence, the basic process of religion, is to take the individual back into his eternal relatedness to the universal. Theologically, it is said that it is the great quest for God. And thus here, this aspect of Yoga is brought out very clearly, when Patanjali said that the success in such concentration may also be brought about by devotion to God and that devotion to God can lead you to Samadhi. Here, he devotes a Sutra to define what the concept of God is.

God is the Supreme Being who transcends this world-process, who is not caught and enmeshed, an ever-liberated Supreme Principle that transcends the world-process, independent, beyond all possibilities of ignorance. It is the nature of pure Jnana or Knowledge. It is all the contrary to our present consciousness. Our consciousness is limited by the finite objects of a temporary nature. Our consciousness is coloured by ignorance, false perception. This Being is of the very nature of pure Jnana or Knowledge, whereas man also has knowledge, but he has got only limited knowledge. Patanjali says that God is unlimited, infinite Being characterised by infinite wisdom, transcending the world-process, a Being in a state of absolute independence, a liberated Being. That is his definition of Isvara, God.

Through devotion to God, Samadhi can be attained. How to practise this devotion? What is this means? The best way of this devotion is used as a means of attaining success. The best practice is constant repetition of the name that symbolises Him, name that indicates Him, with contemplation upon its meaning, contemplation upon its implication. This name that symbolises the universal Deity, not the God of any specific religion, but the God of universal religion, the God beyond all religions, he gave as 'OM'. And Om is the symbol of the Supreme Being and the repetition of Om with the meaning, is the sure means of attaining success in concentration and overcoming obstacles, which destroys all obstacles. It invokes a special prayer to the Infinite, which is an effective means to overcome the obstacles enumerated. Then, specific types of concentration to overcome these obstacles were also suggested.

You turn away from gross, sensual pursuits. But what happens, the habit is there. You will have to make special efforts to eliminate them. Then alone you would be able to turn away from those gross, sensual pursuits. If you relax a little bit, once again the mind goes back into its own ruts, old sensual habits. This is another obstacle. Due to this tug-of-war, seesaw of your struggle with your inner nature, despair comes. Because you fail many a time, you become hopeless. Never despair. Always one should have hope—'I will overcome them, come what may.' You may get nervous. Nervous condition may come to the practitioner; trembling and even irregularity of breathing. And to overcome all these things, without being a psychiatrist, Patanjali has got different methods of concentration. This is his prescription.

One is, of course, to make up his mind—'No matter what comes, I am not going to leave this quest which I have taken up.' So, Patanjali prescribes Ekatattva-Abhyasa—catching hold of some one type of practice and clinging tenaciously to it and never letting it go, come what may. Ultimately, this overcomes all the obstacles. It is an exercise of the power of one's determination, inner will, and invoking a positive state of mind, always keeping the mind in a cheerful and positive state.

So, he prescribes four patterns of reacting to the outer world. Kumbhaka or retention of the breath is one of the important methods to overcome the obstacles. And no one method alone is supposed to be used. Selected, judicious combination of more than one method may be suitable to you. As a result of study of your own nature, special exercises which bring about some immediate result may act as good encouragement. Meditation upon the inner light of the Atman and meditating upon, contemplating upon the Masters, saints, sages, Yogins and Gurus, give fresh enthusiasm to the mind and fill you with the spirit of elation, and they become, as it were, inspirers. They give you a new spirit on the path. By contemplation upon deep sleep and dream state you become aware of the dream-like nature of the outward phenomenon. And finally, you can meditate upon anything that attracts your mind, anything that is specially pleasing to you, any symbol or any form. This practice will ultimately lead on gradually and progressively to the state of highest transcendental superconsciousness, highest state of non-dual Samadhi which is beyond the earlier stages described by Patanjali.

Kriya Yoga

Now, Patanjali moves on to the practical aspects of Yoga. Having described most of the earlier concepts of Yoga—trance, concentration, mind-activities, etc.,—he now goes to Sadhana.

Sadhana means any practice as such. Many of you may be aware of the name Ashtanga Yoga, the Yoga of eight limbs. You will be surprised that the Sage does not straightaway launch into consideration of Sadhana in the serial order, i.e., starting from the first stage, going into second and third etc. He does not do it. He first gives the description of what he calls preparation of the ground. Preparation of the ground is positive and negative. It prepares your mind and at the same time, takes away the obstacles to it. Then, he goes on to describe the actual Ashtanga Yoga. In between these, there are a number of Sutras dealing generally with different concepts of the philosophical background of Yoga. We will not directly concern ourselves with them in the present talk. The preparation, he says, is most important and he calls it Kriya Yoga.

This is the working method that leads to the actual Yoga. Tradition has it, that actual Yoga commences, some say, from the fifth and some say from the sixth limb of Yoga. It is rational to keep it as the fifth. The first four are called the outer Yoga and the last four are called the inner Yoga. The outer Yoga is regarded by some as the preliminary preparations for the actual inner Yoga proper. But in the Sutras of Patanjali, he himself mentions the preparations as the second stage of Yoga. So the second chapter of the Yoga Sutras is captioned the 'Sadhana Chapter'. It starts with the aphorisms on: Tapas, Svadhyaya and Isvarapranidhana (austerity, study and dedication to God, respectively). They comprise Kriya Yoga. They comprise the preparatory practices. It is worthwhile considering here, what these three imply, and how exactly and why they are said to be the preparatory practices. Patanjali's Kriya Yoga is austerity, study and dedication to God.

Tapas (Austerity)

What is Tapas? The word Tapas has no exact translation in English language. Though there are many words which may be regarded as giving a partial meaning, yet none of them brings out or connotes the full meaning of this word Tapas. Tapas means generation of heat. Tapas is heat, intensity of heat actually. In Western language, we may say, it means penance, mortification or discipline. Tapas is penance, but penance is not all Tapas. Tapas is mortification, but mortification is not all Tapas. Tapas is austere way of living, but austerity itself is not the goal of Tapas. Tapas means restraint of the senses, control of desires and the diversion of the energy thus conserved towards the subtle process of intense meditation. The energy that is necessary for intense concentration and meditation is to be got by conservation of the same which is otherwise frittered away in diverse directions in various sense-pursuits. Energy is not to be allowed to fritter away. The senses are determinedly held in check. There is a restraint over the desire-nature. This conserved energy is channelled and diverted into the higher, subtle and intense process of concentration and meditation. In this act, a twofold result can be obtained. One is conservation of energy and the second is the purification of the nature of the individual. Because, he puts a stop to gross pursuits, activities of the senses, his nature becomes purified. There is a certain refinement brought about in the nature of the individual. So, it is a purificatory process, just as anything put into fire becomes purified. And this self-restraint by the seeker, naturally creates a tension within him. This energy conserved, you try to leash it and try to give it another direction. So, there is a confrontation between the power of will of the individual and the natural tendency of the urges in man, and this tension brought about with these two aspects of your personality, naturally creates a sort of fiery state. There is heat. Therefore, we have the significant term Tapas.

Svadhyaya (Study)

Svadhyaya is study. It means spiritual study, study of spiritual books, which include philosophical works, the stories of saints, as well as teachings of illumined sages and spiritual teachers. Now, there is in vogue a practice among all major religions, viz., routine reading of scriptures. It is there in Eastern as well as Western religions. There are people, who devotedly, every day, have a routine reading of the Bible. There is a big Bible and they read half an hour every day and then the book-mark is shifted to the latest position, and the book is closed and kept. Next day, some other persons open it and again read a little and the book-mark is shifted. But Svadhyaya is not mere reading.

Svadhyaya is a deliberate study, with attention to the meaning, of what one is studying, so that one is actually absorbed in what is being studied. Therefore, there is every day a fresh intake of spiritual ideas into the mind, into the consciousness. These spiritual ideas are not only informative but also inspirational, as well as of a transforming nature in their effect upon the mind. There is another specific purpose behind the study—we will come to it presently. Svadhyaya means the study with attention on the meaning with the specific purpose of taking in and absorbing it.

Isvarapranidhana (Dedication To God)

It is a term in Sanskrit which literally means placing oneself in God, keeping oneself with constant awareness of the presence of God here and now. It also means the awareness that I dwell in Him, because He is the infinite, the all-pervading One and He dwells in me because He is the indwelling Consciousness of my being as well. Naturally, this implies an unbroken remembrance of the Divine. Elaborating upon the meaning of Isvarapranidhana, Patanjali also goes on to say, how it also implies living for Him, a living for God. That means, you have the conviction that whatever you are doing here, you are not doing for the world; whatever you do, even your secular activity, even duty to your beloved ones, you do it for the love of God and to please Him. Because He has placed you in the particular circumstance, He has put before you the duties. Whatever you are doing is because He has put you in this particular position now, and so it is His Will. Therefore, in fulfilment of His Will you have the full conviction: "I am Thine, all is Thine, I am Thy servant. Therefore, my highest privilege is to carry out Thy Will, and fulfilment of Thy Will; and, I do all this as a method of carrying out Thy Will for me in this life." This also becomes a means of adoring Him, worshipping Him by carrying out His Will upon earth. Isvarapranidhana sums up all these things—living for Him, doing whatever you do for the Will of Him and enjoying yourself in activity in fulfilling the duties of secular life also as doing His Will.

They remove those inveterate tendencies in the individual, with the basic ignorance which stand as bar to illumination. What are these tendencies in human nature, which stand as bar to illumination? One is spiritual ignorance, second is egoism, third and forth, attachment and aversion, and fifth, clinging to life. What is ignorance? Ignorance is characterised by non-discrimination, failing to discriminate between the Eternal and the non-eternal, between the Real and the unreal, between appearances and Reality, between the passing, the perishable and the Permanent, the Imperishable. It is the failure to distinguish between the two and taking the unreal for the Real. Taking the non-eternal for the Eternal—this is ignorance. And regarding the non-self to be the Self, failing to distinguish between the Atman and Anatman, Self and non-self, failing to distinguish between your Self and the body you dwell in and thinking I am this body— this is ignorance, this is spiritual ignorance.

Para And Apara Vidya
(Secular And Spiritual Knowledge)

One may have a tremendous amount of secular knowledge, one might have gone through the university courses and taken several degrees, may be a Ph.D., may be a M.A., a Post-graduate in Science, Chemistry and Mathematics or Commerce. Whatever it is, yet spiritually, one may be totally an ignorant being. For, the acquisition of information about the material world and the things therein, does not in any way help to remove from your inner consciousness, this wrong notion that fails to distinguish between your true Self and that which is only an Upadhi or an added, additional, limiting adjunct that happens to be associated with you and with which you happen to be related—to the body, senses and mind. They are all limiting adjuncts. They are not the true Self but something added on to It temporarily. No amount of secular knowledge can effectively remove this ignorance. Only spiritual knowledge can remove this ignorance. So, from the Yogic point of view, secular knowledge which is utilitarian, which has a pragmatic value, doubtless, is regarded a lesser knowledge. And the knowledge of the Reality which you are, the truth about the real state of your relationship with body and mind, that knowledge which brings you Self-realisation and liberates you from the involvement in this world-process—that is called the higher Knowledge, the greater Knowledge. Knowledge of everything here is the lower knowledge.

Knowledge of the true Self creates in the human consciousness an identification with that which is the Self. Because you are ignorant of your true Self, you become identified with the non-self losing the awareness: 'I am merely dwelling within the body and I am not the body.' Your consciousness has now assumed the state: 'I am the body.' So, this 'I', this human 'I', always knows of itself in terms of race, in terms of sex, in terms of religion, in terms of nationality, in terms of family. So it says: 'I am a European,' 'I am a Chinese,' 'I am a Japanese,' 'I am an Asiatic,' 'I am a Negro,' 'I am an American,' 'I am an Englishman,' 'I am a Frenchman,' 'I am an Italian,' 'I am a German,' and 'I am so and so.' And then the 'I' identifies itself with each of these limiting adjuncts. So, the infinite, untrammelled, true Consciousness, beyond time, beyond space, reduces Itself to a single individualised unity, completely bound up with this body, its sex, its age, its height and its weight. So, this little I-consciousness is always referred to in terms of all these several limiting adjuncts, and yet one feels quite happy about it. One revels in it. One wants to be in it. One clings to it and if some one has a tendency to say anything uncomplimentary to it, one is prepared even to fight for it, for this little 'I'. So, this 'I' which is caught up by this little trap of a body, its age, its height, its weight, its colour, holds your consciousness and yet you are not at all conscious about it.

In spite of all our philosophical study, our consciousness still remains bound by the ego and the senses, and this they call Dehadhyasa. This means, we are identifying with the body and this identification is with one body to the exclusion of all else. Everything else in the universe is external to this egoism. This is the second terrible obstacle, the ego. Out of this ego, come love and hate, aversion and attachment—attachment to this body, attachment to all things that are this body's, i.e., my son, my daughter, my father, my property, my house, my motor car, and so on and so forth. This is out of basic ignorance and the ego. Where there is attachment there is always aversion. So, attachment and aversion go together.

You are attached to many things that are necessary for the body, that the body wants and that the body wishes to keep and enjoy. So, there comes clinging to life. You cling to life because the objects provide pleasant experiences to the body. Everything becomes very real, very important, because, it is very pleasing to the body. One does not want to lose one's life. So, these are the obstacles which stand in the way of illumination and become a bar to concentration and progress towards superconsciousness. Patanjali says that Tapas, Svadhyaya and Isvarapranidhana are the effective methods in removing these obstacles. How? Tapas, self-restraint, subdual of the senses, is an effective way countering one's identification with the body. We are automatically identifying ourselves with all the inclinations to the body and inclinations to the senses. The senses want fulfilment of supply of pleasurable experience. The eyes want to see nice things, the tongue wants to taste nice things, the sense of touch wants to enjoy soft, silky and pleasant touch; the same with the ear, the same with the nose. Austerity counters this tendency of the body by saying: 'No, I will subject myself to utter simplicity of life; I will refuse to give soft and nice feelings to the sense of touch; I will refuse to give too much of tasty things to the sense of taste. In this way, a direct denial of satisfaction to senses by self-imposed discipline of various kinds, imply Tapas or austerity.

This is an effective way of confronting and contradicting the body-identification which tries to manifest itself, to express itself in the urge to fulfil its sense-inclination. So, Tapas contradicts in a direct and effective way and in a practical way, this identification with the body. It is only when you are willing to accept as a working hypothesis, the philosophical concept 'I am not the body, I am different and distinct from the body and separate from the body,' you will not be subject to the tyranny of the body and senses. You can be an unattached witness and refuse to fulfil the demands of the body and senses. It is only when you are willing to accept this hypothesis based upon your conduct and relationship towards the body and dealings with the body, you are able to practise Tapas. Tapas itself implies a willingness on the part of the seeker to set aside the wrong hypothesis that 'I am the body,' and now you base yourself upon this right hypothesis of truth—'I am not the body, I am the Soul, I am the Spirit, I am the Atman. Therefore, I refuse to give the demands of the body and I shall now practise this refusal and manifest this refusal in the form of austerity, denying the senses of their fulfilment.' So it counters this basic ignorance and the attachment and the ego-identification with the body. Svadhyaya is a very efficacious and unfailing means of removing the three obstacles, i.e., ego, love and hate.

Raga And Dvesha (Attachment And Aversion)

These are the products of ignorance. Ignorance creates the ego and the identification with the body. The egoism that results out of ignorance creates attachment and aversion. Therefore, to counter it, try to keep the mind always fed with wisdom, fed with knowledge. Daily study of the Upanishads, philosophical works, study of the teachings of the illuminating Masters bring about revolution in the mind and a transformation in the line of thought which the mind tends to follow.

It has always been tending to think in terms of ignorance, think wrongly, think erroneously. Here, every day you expose it to the light, the light of wisdom. These basic scriptures are the sources of wisdom and therefore the inveterate age-long trend in the mind is turned into new channels of thinking. You create new trends of thinking. The mind begins to think now upon new lines, on lines of new view of things. Gradually the habits of ignorant thinking are replaced by habits of wise thinking. Wisdom now begins to characterise the mind. The immediate effect of Svadhyaya is the removal of ignorance from the mind and bringing in of the light of wisdom, so that now, mind begins to think in terms of Jnana, in terms of spiritual wisdom and the thought-flow is directed in a new direction. It no longer flows towards: 'what shall I eat?' 'how shall I acquire newer and newer experience in this world?' etc. Instead of thinking upon these lines, mind begins to think: 'How can I liberate myself from this world-process?' 'How can I put an end to this body-idea? How can I shatter the ignorance? How shall I enter into the state of Selfrealisation, God-experience? How will I experience that emancipation, liberated consciousness?' In this way, the mind begins to think in these lines and its thoughtprocess now becomes characterised not by the previous ignorance but by wisdom.

Svadhyaya and Isvarapranidhana effectively counter the last of the spiritual obstacles, this clinging to life. You cling to life thinking that the world is real and all the obstacles have real value. Therefore, they assume an exaggerated importance in your life and effectively close you up from higher ideals. If you want to counter this and successfully overcome this world-appearances, then practise Isvarapranidhana. Dedicate yourself to God and not to the things of this world. 'God, that is my true value; that is what I seek; compared to Him all these things are mere straw, of no value whatsoever,' convinced thus, you replace your sense of value, change your sense of value. God becomes to you the central value, the greatest thing in your life and you no longer try to get any meaning in your life in terms of people here or experience here. The tragedy of human life is that we try to make meaning out of something which is basically meaningless. For, all things in the end conclude in death. The things which you thought once as very important now become like dream-objects. Philosophical scriptures admonish always: 'O man! Consider this life. How brief it is, a thing of two days! Alone you come and alone you go. No one follows you when you go. Empty-handed you come, and you go empty-handed. What can you take from here! Even a rusted needle will not follow you when the time comes for your departure. You commit so many sins and make so many enemies, hurting so many people and speaking so many lies. You try to gather things of this earth. Have you considered that even a bit of a rusted needle will not come with you? For this, you bring yourself this bondage of Karma, bring so many bad things. No, no, it is not worthwhile.' All things that are here have to be left in this plane only. Therefore, what have you put for yourself beyond? Have you tried to earn something that will be with you, come with you, something which is of lasting value, enduring value? Think in this way. If you try to philosophise, gradually it tries to bring about a different vision of things. The eternal, the enduring Reality, and not the passing phenomenon, becomes of real value. You begin to live not for the world. You no longer commit the same blunder of trying to find meaning in life in terms of things here.

You try to find a meaning in life in terms of the eternal Reality, when life becomes full of meaning. It becomes the means for the attainment of the great end. It becomes a rare opportunity given to us in order to be utilised, where you can discipline yourself; where you can train yourself; it will become a training ground. It becomes of great value and you look at all things from a different angle. Every experience you now make, becomes a spiritual exercise, something to learn, something to gain more strength inwardly. This something equips you for that supreme attainment. Then life becomes meaningful.

If an individual tries to see whether there is any meaning in life in terms of things here, he will suddenly find that all things are meaningless, because everything is temporary here, everything is changeful. One day everything has to be left. There is no ultimate meaning in life. Great empires have risen and disappeared, great kings have come and ruled and they have vanished. Not even their memories in the minds of humanity exist today. They have been reduced to only little, little sentences in the pages of history books and school books. We read about them in textbooks. Where the great Roman emperors once ruled, now you see only old ruins of amphitheatres and all such other places of interest. What is there? Nothing, wilderness. Jackals howl there at nights, spiders weave their webs, where once upon a time, the Royal Roman emperor held sway. If you reflect over history, you will see how it is all an empty vanity. We are thinking that great important things are happening in the 20th century. After a couple of hundred years, no one will even remember that we existed and we had our big problems and we did huge things. It is all emptiness. When the past is considered, it looks so very silly. In a short while, all this present also will be over, and not one being will be here upon the stage; a new humanity will have this stage in control. We will become their objects of memories. And so, philosophically, if you think deeply, you begin to understand that the ultimate value lies not in this life.

The great Master of Nazareth, Jesus the Christ when he taught, "Seek ye first the Kingdom of Heaven and all these things shall be added unto you," and "What availeth a man if he gained the whole world but loses his own soul," he gave priority for the Eternal, priority for that which is permanent and enduring and not for the passing. The passing has no sense of value. Now, with the shifting of the sense of value, this clinging to life is overcome and by living for God, living for the Eternal and seeking true meaning in life only in terms of that great goal, that ideal, you begin to live now for the goal of your meditation and your Yoga processes, and whatever action you do, you begin to find new meaning in them only in terms of that great ideal. You do all these activities to Him who is ever present, the all-pervading, invisible Essence, the support of all that is. This is Isvarapranidhana. These then therefore, effectively counter and obliterate the obstacles to illumination, which are in the form of ignorance, egoism, attachment, aversion and clinging to life.

Austerity and Svadhyaya remove your basic ignorance and take away this false identification with the body. They explode the myth of this ego and overcome attachment and aversion, by flooding your mind and heart with spiritual wisdom day by day. Regular Svadhyaya, feeling and practising the presence of God, dedicating your activities to Him and living for God, effectively liberate the Consciousness from false, wrong clinging to this worthless life ephemeral, transitory life and put before your consciousness the supreme value of God. This is the fruit of Svadhyaya. These three, viz., Tapas, Svadhyaya and Isvarapranidhana, prepare the ground first, and later on, put before us the eight limbs of Yoga.

Pancha Kosas (The Five Sheaths)

The eight limbs of Yoga are based upon Patanjali's study and understanding of the real inner structure of man, the inner occult structure of man which seems to be a component of five sheaths enfolding the real Being, the inner spiritual essence. The five sheaths are this physical body which is the food-sheath; the inner, biological life-force which is the vital sheath; the sheath of thought and desire, sentiment and emotion which is the mental sheath; the discriminatory rationalistic aspect of the inner being made of intellectual process, reasoning power which is the wisdom-sheath or intellectual sheath; and that sheath made up of the subconscious mind where the residual potencies of previous experiences, subtle, residual potencies or Samskaras and the intricate tendencies created by Samskaras, are lodged. That subconscious mind is the ultimate sheath. It is called Karana Sarira which is the cause of bondage. Karana Sarira is also called the bliss-sheath. Because, in the subconscious, you are not aware of the painful experiences of phenomenal world and so being free from the painful experience of this phenomenal world, that sheath has been named the bliss-sheath where there is no pain and no suffering. These five sheaths are the enfolding factors, holding within themselves, the real spiritual essence. You indwell these five sheaths. Man's real essence is spirit and this spirit is not cognised because it is completely buried under these five coverings, and to approach this spirit, these five coverings have to be disciplined and brought under control. The impurities in them have to be removed so that these sheaths do not become obstructing factors but become helping factors to take you inside. They themselves become the helping factors, and this is Yoga.

Yama And Niyama

The body, the first grossest sheath, is the physical sheath. It is seen in manifestation through its activities. Patanjali states in his Yoga Sutras, that you should bring about a transformation in your activities. And he effectively does it by committing the seeker, first of all, to five principles, and these principles are:

1. Abstaining from causing injury (Ahimsa)
2. Abstaining from falsehood (Satya),
3. Abstaining from sexual licence (Brahmacharya),
4. Abstaining from theft (Asteya), and
5. Abstaining from luxury (Aparigraha).

To abstain from these five things is the first stage in the discipline of Yoga.

And I will close this talk of today by telling you that with regard to these five principles, Patanjali says that there is no excuse, there is no exception and there is no special circumstance where you may be let off, where you may relax from these. These are the universal vows which a Yogi must fulfil, no matter in what circumstances he is, where he is, and in what condition he is. In any context, he must fulfil them. So, any consideration of special time or place or circumstances does not release him from these vows. They have to be observed at all times, in all places, under all conditions and under all circumstances. This, he specially insists upon. Are there any exceptions to these? He says that if you really want to enter into a state of Yoga and be a spiritual seeker, there is no exception to these. You may say: 'I am not able to fulfil them properly, I am failing.' That is all right, but don't say that under these circumstances they need not be observed. So, you admit or confess your failings but do not lower them (the vows) into another level. They are there and they have to be observed in all their fullness. These are the principles that go to make up the first step.

The second step comprises the five observances you have to follow in daily life. The first two are inner and outer cleanliness and contentment. Have a frame of contentment in the mind always. Never murmur, never grumble, never wail and weep. Never accuse people around you. Always be content. Three we have already mentioned, viz., austerity, study and dedication to God. These five comprise the second stage.

Third stage is practising steadying of the body, bringing a state of absolute steadiness in the body, in the posture. The fourth stage is regulating the breath, trying gradually to gain control over breathing through which you gain control over the subtle inner force. These four, concerning themselves as they do with the outer activity of man, the inner observation in daily life, the body and the breath, they are referred to as outer Yoga. From the fifth stage comes the inner Yoga, withdrawal of the mind, concentration of the mind, and entering into a state of continuous, unbroken meditation. These three comprise inner Yogic process leading to the state of Samadhi which we shall take up tomorrow. In our next lecture, we can discuss about the eight graded steps (Ashtanga), after covering which we will more or less get a full working knowledge which will help us to take up to the practice of Raja Yoga in our own life.

God bless you all. May you all shine as perfect Yogins in this very life, in this very body, or at least, may you all try and make sincere efforts to shine as self-disciplined masters of yourself, put an end to slavery and put an end to wrong notions, all wrong notions arising from the delusion of 'I am the body' idea. May the Divine Grace ever be upon you all!

Fifth Lecture:

Asmita, Raga and Dvesha (Egoism, likes and dislikes)

Beloved Immortal Souls! Radiant Atman! Blessed seekers in the path to Perfection!

Welcome to our continuation of our previous talks. Greetings to you all. In our last talk, we briefly touched upon the 1st, 2nd and 3rd Sutras of the second chapter of Patanjali's Yoga aphorisms, that is the chapter on Sadhana. The first Sutra sums up what Kriya Yoga is and in explaining the Sutra, we mentioned how Kriya Yoga according to Patanjali had a specific meaning.

In the classical Yoga aphorisms of Patanjali, Kriya Yoga explains the three disciplines of practice—i) austerity (Tapas), ii) spiritual study (Svadhyaya) and iii) dedication of one's life and activity to Godhead, starting to live for God, feeling His presence at all times and doing everything as an offering to the presence of God (Isvara-pranidhana). These three combined, Patanjali refers to as Kriya Yoga—"Tapa-svadhyaya-isvarapranidhanani kriya-yogah" These three comprise Kriya Yoga and he goes on to say that Kriya Yoga is an effective discipline for helping the seeker in cultivation of concentration and in removing the obstacles to illumination. This is the second Sutra. And, then he mentions briefly, what are the obstacles to illumination in the seeking aspirants or in the spiritual Sadhana. He lists these obstacles as being primarily due to spiritual ignorance and secondly as the outcome of spiritual ignorance.

The finite, separated ego-consciousness, Asmita, arises from wrong or erroneous identification of consciousness with the physical body and the mind. We saw how as the outcome of such an identification, the 'I' consciousness of one's own individuality becomes the most important thing for the individual, that for which he lives and dies. It has really no substance and enduring basis at all, because it is based upon and identified with a particular physical body, and the name-label given by the parents to this physical body at birth cannot have real or enduring basis. This body was not there before its birth, it has appeared at a certain point of time, which means before that point of time this body did not exist. Therefore, this ego-consciousness which is based upon it, also was not existent at that time. It has a very, very unstable, unreliable support of this body.

The name-label given to it was non-existent before the body came into being, and similarly, it again ceases its existence with the death of the body. When the body dies, the name-label given to this body also is annihilated with it, which means, this egoconsciousness ceases to be, the very moment this body ceases to be. Because, it is based upon this body. The result is the identification of this consciousness with one particular body and it takes upon itself all the distinctive and distinguishing marks of the body. Suppose, there is another person of the same label and if some one says 'I met you there,' or some one says 'You were the same person, who appeared there,' he would then say 'no, no, he might have my name, but he is a French man,' or 'He is some one else,' or 'He is not myself, because, I was born in such and such a place, and this is my age while that person is 15 years older to me and he was born somewhere else.' So, we identify ourselves with this body, with its distinct marks and distinguishing features. So, the consciousness becomes identified with an object which has a beginning or a birth, at a certain point in time and which soon ceases to be and goes out of existence at another point in time. Therefore, the life of this ego is only commensurate with or co-existent with the life of the physical body, which means the ego has no real existence. It did not have any existence a little while before, and soon it goes out of existence. So, it is a mere appearance, a temporary appearance in time, and yet this is taken to be the greatest reality. The whole life of an individual is completely terrorised by it, dominated by it and for its sake he is prepared to do anything. He fights, quarrels, does violence, hurts others and creates disharmony, discontent and does anything. Such is the power of Avidya or Ajnana or spiritual ignorance.

An unreality which does not really have any substantial or permanent existence, which has only a temporary appearance for the time being, becomes the factor that dominates the consciousness of the individual and thus holds the consciousness within its infinite bound in a sort of imprisonment. This is Samsara, this is bondage. This is what is called phenomenal existence. This is the outcome of spiritual ignorance. This makes us losing awareness of our true nature, our permanent eternal nature, moving away from our consciousness which is our permanent nature, and identifying ourselves to a temporary appearance. This body is just a temporary appearance, just as a bubble appears upon the surface of water. It was not there a little while before, it appears, and as you are seeing it, it bursts and it is no longer there. In the same way, this body has a temporary appearance upon the surface of eternity, eternal time. Therefore, this is a product of ignorance due to forgetting of one's eternal nature. This ego, having identified itself with the physical body, conceives attachment for it and this attachment is like a creeper which starts to grow at one point and then gradually spreads.

In the same way, Dehadhyasa or identification with one body, this form and this name, gradually concedes attachment to it and this attachment starts extending to all things that are some way or other related to it. 'I am so many years old. This body is mine. Therefore, I am attached to it, and then I am attached to my wife, I am attached to my husband, I am attached to my children, to my brother or sister, to my mother or father, to my friend and to my house, to my wrist-watch, to my fountain pen, to my gold, to my jewellery, to my clothes and so on and so forth. When my daughter grows up, she is given in marriage to some one in some other family. My attachment now goes even beyond the bonds of my family and goes to that other, family also, because, he is my sonin-law, my daughter's husband.' So, in this way, attachment starting from one body goes and spreads to all other persons, objects or situations which are pleasing to the body, desired by the body. Thus attachment goes on. It is called Raga. Raga means conceiving attachment to things of temporary appearance called the world-process.

At the same time, anything that stands in the way of expression of this attachment, anything that stands in the way of our fulfilment of our desires, towards that we conceive aversion. Anything that is not pleasing to the body and the senses, anything that is not mine or anything that stands always in the position of what is not mine, towards that we conceive aversion. As I told you, where there is attachment there is always aversion also. Love and hate go together. If you like sweet things, you do not like bitter things. In this way, the world being made up of duality, if you attach yourself to one set of things or one kind of things, you are averse to the opposite kind of things. If you are attached to late rising, you are vexed to early rising and you don't want it. And if you are attached to over-eating, you do not want to abstain from it and you do not like even to be told about it.

The whole world is made up of what is known as Dvandvas. Dvandvas means pairs of opposites, two things which are mutually opposite to each other. Therefore, attachment to one includes within itself aversion to that which is opposite of it. And this wise being bound by ignorance, clinging to this 'I', attached to wrong identification with one body, thus gives rise to attachment and aversion. In this process of seeking that which one likes and avoiding that which one does not like, this life-process completely absorbs the individual and he clings to it as something very dear to him. The very thought of death, that something which creates fear, that one does not like. So, clinging to life, the fifth obstacle to illumination, springs up. Ignorance, egoism, attachment, aversion and clinging to life can be overcome by the practice of Kriya Yoga. Kriya Yoga removes all these obstacles to illumination. How this is done—we considered in our previous class. Tapas, self-control, self-denial, the restraint of the senses, control of the senses and conquest of desires counter ignorance and its effects.

The identification with the body and the basic ignorance which is the cause for bondage become countered by both Tapas and Svadhyaya. Because, you contradict the identification with the body by denying the senses, by refusing to identify yourself with the senses and the sense-urges, saying 'no, I stand apart from them,' you refuse to cooperate with them. 'I am not the sense-urge. Therefore, I will not give in to them, but stand apart by the unattached witnessing consciousness.' So, you start a counter. Up-till now, life has been flowing in the direction in which the senses were dragging and going along with the mind, in whatever direction the desires pulled you or pushed you. But now Tapas or austerity aids you to refuse to give in to the desires of the mind. You refuse to succumb to the urges of the senses and now you start countering them. See, you start confronting them, approaching them with the power of the will by discrimination. Coming into contact with Yoga philosophy, has brought into your mind, the idea that you are not this body, senses and the mind, and that you are a distinct, ever-free liberated being whose nature is Pure Consciousness,—Existence, Consciousness and Bliss. Therefore, enough of this bondage of the body, senses and mind.

Now you must claim your birthright. You must assert yourself. You must affirm your true nature and thus liberate yourself from this identification and bondage. This truth will come into the life of a seeker through philosophy. Now, he wants to practise this truth. Therefore, Tapas is one of the ways of actually putting into practice the truth, "I am not this body," "I am not this mind," "I am not these senses," "I am not this desire," etc. When this is so, you wish to manifest your distinctive nature and you do this by austerity. Refusing to give in to the senses, refusing to give the desire its objects, creates in the inner psyche, a certain confrontation between the lower mind, the gross senseurges in the individual and the higher awakened discriminative faculty, rational faculty of the individual. This confrontation between gross sense-urges and the higher awakened intellect, rational faculty of the individual, creates a certain tension and this tension guarantees an intense psychic energy within. It augments a fiery will-power, and hence the significant term Tapas. Given to this process of standing confronting and facing your lower nature, that significant term means heat. Energy is generated by this confrontation. So, what happens, this energy is now available to you. If you go along with senses and the desires, your energy fritters away, your energy is expended in sense-experiences, in desire-fulfilments. Now, in as much as you refuse to give in to these lower sense-urges, that energy is conserved and it becomes a valuable asset to you for higher spiritual purposes or techniques of Yoga, concentration and meditation.

The conversion of this energy is done through Pranayama. Pranayama and Asana, both have the power of converting the conserved gross energy into more subtle psychic energy. To some extent, even the various Hatha Yoga postures also have the effect of enabling the practitioner to convert gross physical energy into higher, subtler form of energy. And as you begin to practise Hatha Yoga, this conversion begins to take place. When you go into the Raja-Yogic Asana and Pranayama, this conversion of gross energy takes on a new form. It becomes very refined and starts progressing upward. This process of conversion is called sublimation.

All forms of gross energy including the sex-energy of the individual, are capable of being thus converted into subtler form and then sublimated into a purely psychic energy. And for this sublimated psychic energy, they have a very, very significant and very expressive term in Yogic terminology. They call it radiance or effulgence. The Sanskrit term for it is Ojas. Ojas means radiance or effulgence. So they say, when sublimation takes place, the gross energy-potential of the human being, having been converted into a subtle energy, takes the form of radiance. It is just like a hard piece of ice, for example, which melts and takes on a comparatively or relatively subtler form or lighter form of water and the same thing, when heated and brought to boiling point, becomes still subtler, and rises up in the form of steam. A similar process may be said to happen when the gross physical energy is controlled through Tapas or austerity. Through Hatha Yoga and other Yogic practices, it is converted into a subtler energy. It goes inward and at this stage, it can manifest itself in your nature as good health, strength of the muscles, clarity of the brain, augmented intelligence, and deeper retentive memory. When this energy is controlled through moderation, austerity, it begins to manifest in three forms.

First and foremost, you begin to feel more energetic and begin to see that your health improves and there is a radiance in your complexion and facial appearance; and then the body acquires greater power of resistance to diseases and more stamina to do continued work for a long period of time; and then greater brain-power. It begins to give you the power to have sustained study, sustained thinking and good memory. When it has been converted from gross to subtle and when sublimation takes place, the same power rises upwards and you are able to utilise it for purposes of concentration and inner meditation. It takes up the form of psychic or spiritual dynamism. So, this is the effect of Tapas and this intense heat of Tapas, generated by self-control and conquest of desires, has the nature of awakening within, your awareness of yourself as distinct from the physical body and the senses. So, it counters basic ignorance and bodyidentification. Svadhyaya, i.e., daily regular spiritual study, removes from your nature these second, third and fourth obstacles to illumination, viz., ego-consciousness, aversion and attachment. Because, the material of spiritual study is wisdom, the teaching of the great Masters, and day after day as you go into a serious and earnest study of these books, slowly there comes about a transformation in your mind. Your ignorance is removed, knowledge begins to qualify your thinking and feeling.

Actually, Svadhyaya is a type of negative Satsanga. That means, you put yourself in contact with the great master-minds and spiritual luminaries of the past as well as the present. Because these people were perfected beings, their words are living words. They never die. They are immortal words. For instance, if you take to a regular study of the 'Evangel,' then you begin to live and move with the Divine personality of Jesus day after day. If you begin to read the Gospel in a systematic way, with reverent attitude, with right feeling towards it, what happens is this: It has the effect of moving you from the time-space framework and taking you into a different time-space dimension, and therefore you will be living in the time of Jesus, walking along with him, and remain in his company. You will be transported, may be in the source of Galilee and then you will become one with the audience that drank in his immortal nectarine words. The tyrannical hold of this time-space work will have no meaning for you. You transcend beyond this time-space framework. We make much of the modern times, and think that it is difficult for us to live the Divine Life in this twentieth century. This is all self-created condition. You yourself are creating this condition because you always think: 'I belong to the modern times, I belong to the 20th century, I belong to the West, and this is not possible for me.' This is all ninety per cent self-created conditioning.

Human nature has always been the same. And whatever applied to the human being 5000 years ago, it applies even now also. It will apply to him as long as the sun and moon shine. Because, the inner nature is always the same. Environment must have changed. Outer things must have changed, but the basic human being and his problems have not changed. What he had to struggle against is the same. And therefore, the eternal validity of these teachings that show the way of solving the eternal human problems cannot be questioned. To this self-created tyranny, this conditioning coming out of the environment which has gripped the psychology of modern man, Svadhyaya offers an unfailing, efficacious method of breaking it by giving you a means, a technique by which you completely transport yourself into a different time-space condition. Gradually the exaggerated sense of importance which things, events and environments holds you in their grip, that exaggerated grip or importance is loosened. So, you are in a better position, a position of advantage to deal with them. You can renounce them, you can triumph over them, you can overcome them, because, you have loosened yourself from their bear-like grip. Day after day, if, in this way, you go into deep Svadhyaya what happens? You begin to live and move in the company of those illumined sages like Buddha, like Jesus. Supposing you are absorbed in the study of Gita, every day regularly at a set time, what happens is, you are actually in the company of the great Master Krishna and He is not so much speaking to Arjuna, He is speaking to you. You are receiving the Wisdom-teaching from Him directly.

In this way, Svadhyaya is a marvellous gift of removing from human mind, ignorance and false ego-consciousness, brought about by ignorance and the attachment to passing things and the aversion that follows at the heels of attachment. These three products go to form basic spiritual ignorance. Ignorance is the cause of these three things, viz., false ego-consciousness or individualised ego-consciousness, attachment and aversion. Gradually, you are able to remove them from your consciousness by regular Svadhyaya which is imbibing of wisdom, day after day. You begin to enlighten and illumine your inner being by Svadhyaya and Isvarapranidhana. They remove the last obstacle, this clinging to life. Because, it gives you a totally different sense of value which is no more of this world. All its glittering things have no more importance to you. Because, you begin to replace this feeling and attitude in a different and changed vision. 'I am living for this world with the new attitude, I am living for the Reality, I am living for the universal Being, the Almighty Being, I am living for the Reality, not for the passing unrealities.' That is Isvarapranidhana. It effectively makes you to overcome this clinging to this little life, by bringing you into a different state of mind, where your sense of values is totally transformed and where the goal becomes not anything here, but the Ultimate Reality. You live and move and have your being in God. He becomes the Supreme Value and to attain Him, becomes your goal.

This is the effect of Tapas, Svadhyaya and Isvarapranidhana in relation to the basic obstacles to illumination. There is a monastic tradition of Tapas taking various practices, such as walking without shoes, moving bare-headed, without umbrella in the rain and the sun, and sleeping upon hard bed instead of having soft and luxurious bed, making the diet simplest—mere vegetables, bread and water—occasional fasting, bearing heat and cold, and bearing discomforts without murmuring, without grumbling. These positive acts of mortification, the ancient ones underwent, are unbelievable. Even forgoing things to which the human beings have become accustomed to, the more and more comfortable way of living evolved by modern scientific civilisation—that itself becomes an enough kind of austerity, even without subjecting yourself to the positive, painful mortifications. The very fact of forgoing things to which you have become addicted, accustomed and habituated, that itself has become an act of Tapas. In the physical level, this expresses itself as Tapas.

Svadhyaya unifies the mind and heart by bringing in spiritual wisdom and inspirational spiritual thoughts and sentiments, Isvara-pranidhana—dedication to God—brings your deepest inner being to your Consciousness, the purifying light of God's presence and His Divine Presence, in everything that you do. Now, how do these three things have direct effect upon concentration? Tapas unifies your thoughts and feelings by eliminating from you the excitement and stimulation of constant sense-experiences. Every time, you indulge in sense-experience, it stimulates you, it creates inner excitement and this excitement causes restlessness of the mind. Craving is intensified by sense-experience. So by countering that, by eliminating from your daily life and your experience, the excitement and stimulation of sense-indulgence, Tapas unifies your thoughts and feeling and brings about stability. It also curbs Rajas, the Rajo-Guna which is the factor that causes restlessness in the mind. This is how Tapas has a direct bearing upon concentration, unifying of thought.

Svadhyaya, spiritual study—how does it help in cultivating concentration? What is the field of the activity of the ordinary mind? The whole universe, everything, whatever is seen, heard, touched, tasted or smelt, the object of the five senses, all the world over, is the area. This is the field of wandering of the mind. Because, the desire-nature is predominant in it. It wants everything, anything that it sees, and always keeps on seeing things. Now, Svadhyaya or spiritual study tends to confine the mental activity by offering it a selected field in which it can keep itself revolving. Day by day, your mind is brought into a particular field and kept in that field. Spiritual subject, spiritual material is always given before it. So, it tends to confine the mental activity and thus fix the mind in concentration. Because, this area or field has direct relevance to and is connected with the subject of your inner meditations. Because, it is spiritual study, though the mind wanders, it begins to wander only in that area.

For instance a cow is left loose in the pasture; then it is free and goes on nibbling at everything that is there. It may be good grass or some bush. But supposing you put a peg and tie it to that peg by a rope, what happens is, it is free to a certain extent to the length of the rope. Supposing it is fifty feet length rope, to the length of that rope, it is free to go anywhere; but now it has necessarily to confine its grazing only to that circular area which is within the radius of the rope with which it is tethered and tied to the peg. Now the cow becomes confined to a specific area or field. In the same way, the mind becomes tethered to a specific area of thought-activity. More and more it tends to keep its thought-activity to its area. Thus it helps.

This practice of Yoga now progresses by the systematic following of the Yoga techniques which have been classified into eightfold stages by Patanjali and the eightfold stages partake of a practice of progressive nature, negative and positive. Supposing you try to earn money and you want to increase your wealth, so you have to accumulate. Then it goes on increasing. Supposing, you have in your life such habits that are wasteful. What happens? You exert, work hard to earn more money, and every month as much as you earn, you go on spending. Perhaps, even more, borrowing and spending, and when such a process is taking place, you go on earning and at the same time you go on spending. Can you ever earn and spend and at the same time accumulate! Growing rich not merely implies working hard and earning money, but also implies automatically not wasting it away. Therefore, when you are trying to move towards higher and higher in spiritual stage, concentration and meditation, if in your life, there are leaking loopholes, things which are opposite of it and the contradiction of it, then you are your own enemy. You are working against yourself. You will never amount to anything. There can never be any spiritual progress, let alone illumination or God-realisation. Therefore, first plug the loopholes. Anything that is unspiritual, anything that is undivine, anything that is antithesis, contradiction of what you are going to work for and trying to attain, has no place, has no rational place. Therefore, these things have to be eliminated.

Patanjali ensures that the Yoga way of life is a complete protection of the whole life against all things that are unspiritual and undivine. Therefore, he wants us to avoid violence and cruelty which contradict the nature of God, spiritual Divine nature, love and compassion. They ought to reign supreme in the seeker's life. Therefore, injuring others, untruth and falsehood are unspiritual and undivine. They contradict God, who is Truth. Therefore, abstaining from falsehood is an indispensable prerequisite of the Yoga way of life. The gross carnality, sensuous nature, is a bar to progress towards the spiritual, finer and finer, subtler and subtler states of consciousness. Therefore the seeker should hold in check these propensities. Continence or celibacy is the third principle. According to one's special stage of life, the term celibacy can have two meanings. For the one who has not yet entered into the second stage of life, i.e., married, family stage of life, it means absolute continence, total one hundred per cent abstinence from sex-activity; and for those who have taken to monastic vows, it similarly means absolute one hundred per cent continence. Those who are married and in family stage of life, it means a rational moderation in one's sex-life. It means, therefore, an abstinence in the form of rational moderation. Later on, when he takes up to Yoga practice and starts making a steady progress in Yoga, a stage will come when he also will have to adopt the same meaning as it applies to one who is in the bachelor state and one who is in the monastic stage. But until he has become established in higher stages of Yoga, it has thus a modified meaning. But a control over grosser passions, rational moderation in their exercise—this principle is a must in the Yoga way of life. While Yoga does not totally contradict sex, it does improve upon sense-expression, a certain restraint and moderation and ultimately going into a state of sublimation.

You cannot have greed for transitory things and at the same time, want the kingdom of Heaven. If you want that, you must be joyfully, willingly ready to renounce your desires, renounce your greed and attachment for earthly things. The last two Yamas imply this. Abstinence from theft, greed, cupidity, covetousness unlimited desires—abstinence from these five, therefore, forms the basis. They are safeguards. If these things are not observed, your spiritual life will be like earning thousand and spending thousand, or trying to fill a pot which is full of leaks or holes. It will never get filled. It will only be an effort without any result.

The Parable Of The Oxen

A classical example is given of the oxen at the oil-man's mill, in olden days. The oilpressing was done by oxen. They went round and round, and oil-seeds were put into the centre of the press. In the morning, at sunrise, the oxen used to be hitched to this oilpress and in the evening at sunset, they were unyoked. They cover miles and miles but they do not attain any destination. They are there, where they are. Because, they are bound with the mill. In the same way, an aspirant who is bound to this sensual life, a life of greed, covetousness, sensuality—being bound by these, all his efforts are in vain. They are futile exertion and do not take him to his goal, because, he is bound to the state of lower life. The lower state of life has to be eliminated and hence the first limb or stage of Yoga.

Life is dynamic. It is either progress or regress. It cannot be static. You cannot say: 'I shall just try to be virtuous by not sinning.' You must have enthusiasm for virtues and you must actively express your virtues. Then alone there is freedom from actual sin.

Otherwise, if you say 'I am virtuous by not sinning,' it is only an apparent hypocrisy. Mind will always dwell on sinful things.

May be, you abstain from sinning physically. But the mind is always dwelling there. So, this is only an apparent state of freedom from sin, while actually the person is still in a state of evil and impurity. Therefore, virtue should always be expressed in positive activity. In the same way, these things, these abstinences, self-control and all that, should also be given positive expression.

Saucha (Purity)

The first among the five factors that go to make up the second stage of Yoga is outer and inner purity, purity of outer life, purity of environment. Because, mind is always a creature of suggestions, it tends to think that with which it is associated, or anything with which it is associated even sets up a similar train of thought. Therefore, if you surround yourself in your home by objects of luxury and sensuous pictures and all that, your mind will tend in that pattern of thought and sentiment. If you are surrounded yourself with nice mottoes of elevating masters, with pictures of great people like Mahatma Gandhi, Jesus, Buddha and such other saints, naturally the impact upon your mind will be different. Therefore, outer and inner purity—purity of food, purity of environment, purity of company are very essential if you want to progress in Yoga.

Remember the teachings of Jesus Christ. He said: "He who has cast a sinful eye upon another woman, has already committed adultery." He says action is already there in the mind. Therefore, purity of gaze, purity of sentiments, purity of attitude towards the outer world and things—these are all internal purity.

Santosha (Contentment)

Contentment is very necessary in order to keep your mind optimistic. The dejected and discontented mind is not a fit instrument for concentration and meditation. It should be positive, expanded and cheerful. Contentment leads to the highest type of happiness. The contented man is always cheerful and happy, wherever the Lord has placed him. He knows that in whatever circumstances the Lord places him, he will be happy. He will never grumble and never murmur. He accepts the wisdom of the Lord and remains contented at all times.

Asana (Steady Posture)

The practising of an absolutely steady posture is very essential to progress in meditation. Acquiring a mastery over the body and acquiring the ability to keep the body absolutely steady and unshaken for a protracted period, to assume and maintain a pose steadily and unhurriedly for a long period of time, is a necessary stage in Yoga. Patanjali's definition is 'a control over the body;' though the word Asana comes here, it should not be confused or mistaken with the Yoga Asanas of Hatha Yoga. That is a different type of Asanas. Here, Patanjali means by meditative pose, a specific posture which is conducive to meditation. He says, only two things should characterise it—it should be steady, and it should be comfortable and easy. Otherwise, what will happen? Your mind will be brought to the body, if it is uncomfortable and painful to you.

Why this steadiness of body is insisted upon? I will give you a little idea of the constitution of man, the structure of man according to the Yoga vision. Suppose you have a brass vessel and it is filled with water and in the centre of the water, a big flower, a full bloomed flower is floating. Now, you take a small hammer or some object and hit the vessel of water. When you hit the vessel from outside, you are not touching the water, much less the flower, but the knock you gave to the vessel starts vibrating the vessel. The brass of the vessel begins to vibrate due to this impact and the entire volume of water that is there is set into vibration, ripples are created upon the surface of the water and the whole water takes in the vibration. Vibration is transmitted from the brass material of the vessel into the water that it contains, because, they are in contact. The moment this transmission takes place, the flower which is calmly floating in the centre of it also starts bobbing up and down. So, the motion is communicated to the flower also. This is more or less, the situation with man. The gross body is the receptacle, like the brass vessel. Prana is like the water that fills the vessel. Prana is the biological life force, the vital force, and this biological life force keeps the body alive and animates it. Like the flower kept in the centre of the water, in the centre of the Prana is the mind.

Mind is held in Prana. If the body is dis-co-ordinated or disturbed in its vibratory state, the Prana also will be in a dis-co-ordinate state of vibration and that gets communicated to the mind also. Prana is the centre, it is connected on one side with the body. It is connected on the other side with the mind. Through Prana, this body is connected with the mind and also connected with the body. So, they are inter-connected. The mindactivity and Pranic activity have got a direct connection. If the Prana begins to vibrate, mind begins to agitate with full of thoughts; and if Prana can be restrained, the thoughtprocess of the mind also can be restrained. Pranic vibrations and thought-activity are closely inter-connected. In as much as Prana is held with the body, the vibratory state of the inner body-cells has got a direct relevance and relationship with Prana. It will be a great help if you can bring about a certain conscious control of the inner Pranic movements, inner Pranic activity. This is achieved by Asana. Day after day, if you go on practising Asana, what happens is, the entire vibratory tempo of the inner body-cells becomes gradually stabilised. They assume a state of calmness, serenity and this has to be practised every day without disgust and with unfailing regularity. Then the practitioner can be said to have mastered this state of Yoga.

According to Patanjali, if you can sit calmly and motionlessly, without being disturbed, for a period of three hours at a stretch, you can be said to have mastered the Asana. That is the standard given by Patanjali for those who want to attain mastery over Asana and it is called Asana Jaya. It is not so difficult as it seems, if you know the technique of doing Asana. To sit in an Asana in a steady pose, the only two requirements are: first, your whole body should be totally relaxed and there should not be any tension of any portion of the body and there should not be stiffening of any muscle. One should not try to assume a sort of conscious rigidity in the body. The whole body, all the muscles should be in a state of absolute relaxation and rest—no tenseness, no artificial rigidity and no forced stiffening of any muscle. You must consciously relax the muscles. If you do not relax then it is not perfect. The second requirement is, to keep the head, neck and trunk in a straight line. The back should be Straight. There are two important reasons why these two have to be fulfilled. One is, if you strain any muscle, within a few minutes, it will start aching and your attention will be diverted to it. The second is, if you keep your back straight, two things happen. One is, the body becomes lighter after some practice. It assumes a balance, the centre of gravity is completely in a straight line, and then you don't feel the body. You don't feel that you are sitting at all.

Complete lightness comes to the body. It becomes like a flower, and so, the mind can easily be taken away from the body. The second effect is by keeping the body and the back straight, the chest becomes expanded. It is very very important that the bony cage of the chest should be expanded. If it is expanded, the full volume of breathing becomes easy. So, there is no constraint and congestion in the breathing, and the mind does not go down to the body by irregular breathing. When breathing becomes free and easy, breathing no longer poses a problem. It is no longer an obstacle to inner concentration. So this facilitates taking your mind away from the body. You completely become straight, balanced, weightless; the chest being expanded due to straightness of the back, breathing becomes free and easy, and then slowly the mind is taken away from the body.

Once the mind is taken away from the body, time becomes a minor consideration, whether you sit for half an hour or one hour, it is the same to you. If you acquire complete victory, or full control over the posture, gradually the body becomes immune to heat and cold also. Pain does not affect, heat and cold do not affect. When you have assumed the pose and gained a complete control over the steadiness of the body, the body-cells become calmed. The vibratory tempo of the body-cells becomes Sattvic. It is no more a Rajasic type of vibration. It becomes Sattvic and now this has a sedative effect on Prana. Prana and body being inter-connected, Prana also assumes a certain state of stability. And now body being no longer an obstacle, distracting your mind, you are ready to take up the process of regulation of breath.

Pranayama (The Technique Of Breathing)

The main emphasis is upon retention. Because, when the breath-activity is inhibited, thoughts of the mind also are checked. The retention may be either inhaling and retaining the breath, or exhaling and retaining it, or it may be at any time. When the mind is a little concentrated, it simply retains the breath, whether the breath is in or out, inhaled or exhaled, it does not matter. Actually, at any state of respiration, simply retain the breath, and check it. This is a great help to concentration. Go on practising. This Pranayama should be practised over a long period of time. As you go on practising steadiness of body, the quality of concentration will gradually improve. And as the quality of the concentration begins to improve, breath comes under your control, and vice versa. Check the breath and the mind stops. Make the mind concentrated outwardly and inwardly, then also the breath comes under check, under control. This is Bahiranga Yoga.

In the next class, I shall start dwelling briefly upon the result of each one of these practices according to observation and experience. What is the result of abstaining from injury or violence? What is the result of abstaining from falsehood? What do you gain from abstaining from incontinence, abstaining from theft and what is the positive gain from the inner and outer purity, from contentment, from Tapas, Svadhyaya and Isvarapranidhana. If they are carried over a certain period of time, positive effects accrue to the practitioner. He starts with that and then goes into the inner Yoga.

Main emphasis is not so much on techniques but it is on practice. There are various Hatha Yogic Pranayamas. But in Raja Yoga, Pranayama only means restraint of the breath, because, it is only with a view to help the concentration of the mind.

May God bless you and may you attain happiness through the regular practice of Yoga.

Sixth Lecture: the Essence of the Four Yogas

Radiant Immortal Souls! Beloved children of Light! Seekers on the path to perfection! Travellers to the shrine of Immortality and Illumination!

You are welcome once again to our little fellowship and sharing. This evening, we briefly touch upon the last talk and then proceed further into the subject.

In our last talk, we briefly considered how Kriya Yoga has direct connection with the main essential Sadhana of Raja Yoga which is concentration and meditation, just as Karma Yoga has with the Yoga of spiritualising all your actions. Every activity becomes directed towards the Divine and every activity, instead of standing in your way as distraction or obstacle or barrier towards God, actually becomes a means of linking you with God, becomes a process of adoration and worship. This is Karma Yoga. This is the Yoga of spiritualising all activities.

In Bhakti Yoga, all your emotions are lifted up to a Divine plane, whereas ordinarily they are active and they operate upon the human plane in all human beings and they are only directed to mundane things and beings. In Bhakti Yoga, you transfer the expression and manifestation of your emotions and sentiments from mundane level to the Divine level. God becomes the object towards which your emotion, your affection, your love and your sentiments are now directed. Thus instead of becoming an entanglement, of becoming a net in which you are caught, it becomes the power to break this net and relieve you and bring you into an internal relationship with the Reality in Its personal aspect. This is Bhakti Yoga.

Jnana Yoga is the Yoga which makes use of the rational power, through the intellect, to cleave through illusion, cleave through the illusion of appearances and which takes you to the Reality which is hidden beyond appearances; and thus it is a way of utilising the power of investigation, observance, enquiry and analysis. In this, the power of the intellect, reasoning becomes the means of liberating yourself from the grip of illusion which is merely the result of non-discrimination or the result of failure to enquire, and making proper enquiry regarding the nature of things which we observe and perceive. Blindly, without enquiring we take them for granted and get involved in them. This path evokes in the seeker the active power of enquiry, Vichara, and out of this philosophical enquiry, right discrimination dawns. Suddenly, you begin to see that things are not just things. They are classified. Something is Eternal and others are non-eternal. So, you begin to discriminate, which is the Permanent and which is impermanent, appearance and the Reality, Eternal and the non-eternal, the Self and non-self.

Right enquiry leads to right discrimination and from discrimination arises right knowledge. Then, you begin to clearly see that some of these are just appearances, passing, unstable and changeful. You begin to feel: 'what a folly to run after these shadows; why not I go after the substance?' So right enquiry and right discrimination gradually create within the consciousness, dispassion, turning away from futile desires for shadows. Thus discrimination leads to dispassion which turns the being towards the quest after Reality, quest after the Eternal. This is Jnana Yoga.

In the same way, Raja Yoga is the Yoga that makes use of the powers of the mind and the will. They purposefully overcome the basic tendency of the mind to go outward and then control and overcome it fully and divert the flow of thoughts within. They make it turn inward and arrest the ceaseless, restless mind-stuff and make the mind-stuff concentrated and direct the concentrated mind towards the ideal that is to be realised. Then, this concentrated mind thus directed towards the ideal through continuous practice, is made to flow in an unbroken stream of concentrated thought upon a single idea. When it reaches this state, it is characterised by the state of meditation and the meditation becomes deep and intense. The last vestige of non-discriminating knowledge of oneself as some one in connection with the phenomenal ego, gets erased and that one attains the state of pure discriminating knowledge when one knows of oneself as being truly distinct and different and apart from all the objects of perception, all that is Prakriti, all that is non-self.

Our perception is not clear. There is knowledge but the knowledge is not precise. In a state of highest concentration and meditation, clarity comes in knowledge. This clear knowledge is characterised by the highest type of discrimination—discrimination between the Supreme Seer and all that is seen, all that is an object of perception including one's own body, senses, thoughts and all intellectual process. One becomes sure of oneself by discriminating oneself as apart from those that go to make up Prakriti, in one's own personality. This is the ultimate result of Raja Yogic practice. It is, therefore, the path of concentration and meditation. But the prerequisite for concentration and meditation is, first of all, changing the flow or direction of the mind inward. As long as it is outgoing, objectward, it is not possible to concentrate at all. It can be concentrated outside. This won't be unified concentration. Therefore, absorption, withdrawing the mind within, is an essential aspect of

Yoga and with this absorption of the mind commences the inner Yoga and it is called Pratyahara.

Pratyahara (Withdrawal)

Pratyahara is withdrawal or abstraction. We saw how Raja Yoga has a direct effect aiding the Yogin to progress in concentration and control of the mind. Tapas aids in concentration, by eliminating Rajas and Tamas. Tapas forcefully restrains the senses. Because, as long as the mind is friendly with the senses and it is willingly related and bound up with the senses, its natural tendency is to flow along with the senses. Senses are always active, because that is their Dharma. It is the inveterate tendency of the eye to open and see. It cannot remain closed. If there is sound, it immediately wants to see what is happening there. And it is the inveterate tendency of the ear to hear. All the senses are made that way. They follow their Dharma. Each one follows its tendency, and the mind being completely with the senses, what happens is, it also flows along with the senses, outside towards the objects ever seeking new experiences and always wanting something. It does not want to remain without change. It does not like monotony. And you have to do any one of the two things: either you have to stop the outer movement of the senses by forcibly restraining them, or you have to talk to the mind and make it understand that its close connection and relationship with the senses is not good for it, that it is not going to bring it happiness and that it will only take it into more trouble, and thus pursue it to give up its connection with the senses.

Tapas does the first thing. It forcefully curbs the senses. It is denying the senses from fulfilling their urges. Svadhyaya does the second thing. It goes on talking to the mind. It goes on putting sense into the mind, putting wisdom into the mind, and goes on attracting the mind to the higher ideal and not being sensuous but supersensuous. How? By placing before it in glowing and thrilling terms, the inspiring examples of lives of saints, the lives of spiritual seekers, those who have gone before you on the path and the wonderful result of such turning away from the senses and moving towards the spiritual. So, in glowing terms, the beauty, the grandeur and the glory of the attainment are put before the mind and thus within the mind is created a new desire for higher things. 'Why should I go after this little thing? Why not I go after something which is grand and glorious?' Thus, a strong aspiration is created in the mind by putting before it the grandeur and glory of the supreme attainment before which all sense-experience pales into insignificance, so much so, the mind feels to give them up as nothing. 'I am going to get a hundredfold, a thousandfold, more than what I am giving up and so why not I give up little, little things?' In this way, the mind is presented with tremendous attraction of the glorious goal and it is made to turn away from its alliance with the senses. This is done through Svadhyaya.

So, the first aspect of it, Tapas does. It puts the axe to the senses. And Svadhyaya does the work of persuading the mind, holding before it the grandeur, glory and beauty of the attainment, putting wisdom into it. These are higher processes. Somehow, you could gradually train the senses and discipline them, make the senses themselves give up their inveterate habit of going towards objects, and follow this new nature that the mind has developed. Because, at this stage, you see, when the mind has developed discrimination, a higher understanding and a desire for the goal, and the senses continue to have their old inveterate tendencies and habits, what happens? There is a two-way pull created in the nature of the seeker—the mind gradually tending to take him up higher but the senses continuing to have their own age-old habit. Therefore, there is within the aspirant a struggle. Will he now listen to the mind or will he overcome the drag by the senses? Why not resolve this struggle? Why not make the senses also follow, as it were, the same nature of the mind? If this is done, it would be the best of all the methods.

Superior to both Tapas and Svadhyaya would be to make the senses your friend. Make the senses also take on to new habits. It will remove all old habits. If this could be done, that would be the best. And this training and gradual discipline for this progress by which the senses are made to renounce their age-long habit, take upon themselves a new habit, as it were, in following the awakened mind. The mind which has now acquired discrimination, and accepted to turn its direction from the world of objects to the world of God, and if the senses also begin to follow the mind, then one is rewarded. This state is brought about by the discipline of Pratipakshabhavana. A very happy analogy is given by the commentator of the Sutras to bring home this new relationship between the mind and the senses. Up till now, the senses were dragging the mind out but here we have a new situation when the mind drags the senses in. Mind now begins to put its influence upon the senses. And the senses are prepared, readily and willingly to follow the mind. A beautiful analogy is brought about to explain this state of affairs—the analogy of the beehive.

The Parable Of The Bee

When all the buzzing bees are going in all directions, here and there, if the queen bee is somehow induced to go in one particular direction, then immediately all the other bees automatically tend to follow the queen bee. Suppose the bee-keeper is trying to shift the hive, change the hive of a certain batch of bees. As long as he is trying to get the bees by themselves, he does not succeed. So, what he does? He takes up the queen bee and puts it upon the new hive, and lo, the trick is done! All bees just follow the queen bee and settle down upon the new hive. The commentator says, in the same way, the senses are made to follow the mind, follow the nature of the mind now, as the bees are induced to follow the queen bee. And this is Pratyahara.

Now, this Pratyahara you must understand. It is not merely a technique. Asana is a technique. You sit and try to train the body into a state of perfect stillness, motionlessness and this is a powerful method of gaining complete control over the Rajas in your system. Because, already by Yama and Niyama, the Tamas has been wellcontrolled, well brought into your control. It has been overcome and the entire nature of the aspirant has become purified. He follows strictly the path of good conduct, and noble character and his daily life is spiritualised by Saucha, Santosha, Tapas and Isvarapranidhana.

Easy Meditative Posture

Rajas is the next formidable quality to overcome. Asana and Pranayama, both of them effectively overcome Rajas. Asana, especially, is made to overcome Rajas and then facilitate and taking up of steadying and arresting of the Prana. Hatha Yoga is also a valuable means to support the practice of Raja Yoga. Because, it has precisely this effect of eliminating Tamas, controlling Rajas and increasing Sattva. But in Raja Yoga, the Asana is intended to maintain a single meditative pose steadily, and at the same time fully relaxed and easy. It should not be a strain upon the one who is sitting. There should be no tension. It should not impose any type of strain.

It should be easy and comfortable. Therefore, steadiness and comfort, these two characteristics are brought into the aphorism that refers to Asana—*Sthiram-sukhamasanam.* Sthiram means steady and Sukham means easy and comfortable. The main thing is to observe to keep the spinal column straight, head, trunk and the neck in a straight line. If this is done properly, then the Asana becomes very light and easy. You no longer feel that you are sitting. There comes a perfect balancing of the centre of gravity of the whole body and the spinal column rests upon its base. Also by sitting straight your chest is expanded. If you bend forward the chest becomes contracted. So by sitting straight, the chest-expansion takes away your mind from the breath. Otherwise, if there is a difficulty in breathing, it is a distraction for the practice of concentration. Therefore, by making the chest expanded, you relax. The breathing becomes normal and harmonious.

There is a peculiar and interesting relation between pose and mental condition. In different mental conditions, unconsciously the body assumes different poses. A condition of positive emotion and joy is always expressed with a particular pose, whereas the negative expression of sorrow is always expressed in contracting the body and bending down of the body. This has been observed and referred to by Sri Swami Vivekananda when he speaks about the psychological necessity of sitting straight. He says: you try whenever you sit straight; when the body is straight, the chest is expanded, then the mind is also expanded and you think of noble thoughts, sublime thoughts and it takes you upward. He also says: if you bend forward, the chest-cage becomes closed, then if you try to have noble thoughts, you cannot have them; you can think only small thoughts and the mind can only go in a horizontal plane, it cannot rise to the sublime heights. Try to make experiments for yourself, whenever you find time. It is true—if you sit straight, you can think noble thoughts and if you sit bending you cannot think grandly. There seems to be an immediate connection between the posture and the thought.

The Taming Of The Pranic Energy

There are several kinds of Pranayama in Hatha Yoga, whereas in Raja Yoga, Pranayama is mainly concerned with the retention of breath. This, of course, happens to have an option of three different modes. You can inhale and retain the breath; you can exhale and retain; and you can suddenly retain the breath without any reference to inhalation and exhalation. These are the three modes. Patanjali touches upon briefly all the three essential points in the retention of breath. Prana and mind have a direct connection and all mental activity is supported by certain Pranic activity. Without Pranic activity, there cannot be any mental activity. If the mind is very active, Prana also vibrates intensely, and if Prana vibrates very intensely, mind is put into a state of excitement. Therefore, the bringing into the Prana a certain harmony and balance and stability, has also the same effect upon the mind, can be done through Pranayama. One point we should not miss here and that is, Prana is an invisible and subtle force and what we check here when we do the Pranayama exercise is actually the breath of the nostril and not the Prana. The retained breath, the ingoing and outgoing breath of the nostril should be known to be different from Prana.

There is a different word for the breath in Sanskrit, viz., Svasa. Prana is something subtle and inward. It pervades the whole body from the top of the head to the tip of your toe. The regulation, control and checking of the breath of the nostril is the Svasa that has been mentioned in Pranayama. Because, this is one of the gross outer manifestation of the Pranic energy within. Therefore, when checking and regulating this, the ultimate effect is that you are able to check and regulate the activity of the Pranic energy inside. This is just as when you want to turn a car, you turn the wheels without touching the wheels. You do it by steering it. You turn the steering-wheel and the car turns. In the same way, there is a connection between the breath and the inner Pranic energy, just as steering-wheel and wheels of the car have got connection. In another way also it has been described.

If you want to stop the clock, the technical way would be to stop the hair-spring. The movement of the clock is brought about by the movement of the hair-spring. Because the hair-spring moves, the whole mechanism of the clock is put into motion and that motion is indicated outside by the movement of the second-hand, or the minute-hand. Of course, we did not have the second-hand in good old days. But then if you don't want to worry yourself by opening the clock and stopping the hair-spring, you arrest the movement of the hand, and the whole mechanism comes to a standstill it being indirectly connected with the subtle movement of that little hair-spring also. This is a gross and outside process, the other is a subtle and inside process. The connection between the breath of the nostril and the inner Pranic energy is something like the connection between the hand of a clock with the movement of the subtle, little hairspring of the clock inside the mechanism.

Very recently, Western medical men have stumbled upon this relationship between the mind and the body, which they did not discover so far. They created many of the physical conditions of their patients, sick people in the hospital and ultimately found that they were brought about by their mental states. So, they have now evolved this concept of psychosomatic illness.

Nowadays, as many as fifty per cent of diseases are treated by treating the mind. They are not treated symptomatically. They try to go into the original cause when they are sure that it is some mental state that has brought about such condition. And they have succeeded to a very good extent. But they have not been able to explain, how exactly the mind interferes with the body. Because, they found certain physical conditions are simultaneous with certain mental states. So they have posited a cause and effect connection between the two, worked upon this hypothesis and got the results.

Interrelationship Of Body, Mind And Prana

They are following now that approach and treatment, yet they have no clear idea as to how exactly the mind works upon any particular part of the body and what exactly is this inner diagnosis or inner anatomy. How exactly it functions, they have no clear idea. So it remains unexplained. This is what happens: The mind affects the body, and therefore it is the mental state we try to treat with tranquillisers or sedatives. They don't actually treat the mind, except in certain cases of extreme impact of the mind upon the body, where through hysteria various physical symptoms are brought about. Then, they put the patient in the hands of a psychologist or a psychiatrist. Otherwise, they take recourse either to sedatives or tranquillisers which for the time being, make the mind go into a state of inactivity. Then there is a temporary relief of the physical symptom. But what happens afterwards? Once again when the mind starts activity, when these sedatives and tranquillisers wear off, it goes back again into that state.

The patient is asked to go on swallowing this pill and that pill continuously to keep the mind always in a state of no-activity. That is unsatisfactory. Because, later on these tranquillisers produce side effects. These sedatives also produce side effects. This is another thing. But it is only in extreme cases. For instance, there have been cases where hysteria has brought about an actual state when man becomes crippled. He cannot walk. He loses the use of a limb, or he may get even an attack of paralysis. Hysteria can bring about actual blindness. Person loses his sight. But the psychologist says that there is absolutely nothing wrong with either the eye, or the retina or the optic-nerve or any other thing in the brain-centre. Everything is perfect but yet he cannot see. So, many a time it is found out that a state of shock puts a person into deep hysteria or a state of fear. A soldier has been called for drafting, he does not want to go to war, suddenly he becomes crippled or be loses the power of speech or he cannot use his hand. It is an actual physical condition. But, if he is told: 'all right, you can go home, you are unfit, you are not to be taken to the army,' after going home, he becomes all right. He is able to walk gradually, his hand also begins to move, and speech comes back. So, in such cases, they put him into the hands of a psychiatrist. This abnormal and known fact of interconnection between mind, Prana and body, and the connection between body, Prana, and mind—this answers an unanswered question and explains a hitherto unexplained psychosomatic phenomenon. The mind affects the body through the medium of Prana.

Western doctors admit that many of the physical conditions in the patients are caused by their mental state. But how precisely the mind acts upon the body, they do not know. They have extensively observed, classified and listed all the psychosomatic states. All the physical and mental conditions have the corresponding Pranic pattern. Every physical and mental condition is generated and supported by specific Pranic state in one or other area. This is what is responsible for communicating a mental state to the physical level and for translating it into a particular manifestation there. Even so, physical state also in some cases, has been transmitted to the mind and it has affected the mind.

Benefits Of Yama And Niyama

Now, various Yamas and Niyamas—what gain do they bring for the aspirants? If one becomes absolutely established in Ahimsa or non-injury, he acquires the power to overcome all enmity. To that person, no one can come with anger or hatred. No one can raise the hand of violence. Before him all enmity ceases. If a person who has become perfectly established in Ahimsa goes into the jungle, the moment wild animals come to him, they will become docile. They cannot manifest their violent propensity. That is the result or the effect of acquiring perfection in Ahimsa.

Perfection in truth is Satya. It gives you Vak-Siddhi. If one is absolutely established in truthfulness, then after a period of 12 years of such perfect adherence to truth, whatever the person utters will come out true. And to explain it, Patanjali gives a very interesting form to the Sutras. He says such a one acquires the power of achieving the fruits of action without acting.

One who is established in absolute truth, the moment he utters it becomes truth. It is called Vak-Siddhi. Therefore, a Yogi who becomes established in truth is very careful in what he says. If he curses, the curse turns out true. But of course, a Yogi will never curse because he has overcome anger. If he blesses, the blessing becomes true. It becomes an actual fact in the case of one actually established in perfect truth for a minimum period of twelve years.

Establishment in Brahmacharya brings about superhuman power in the individual, superhuman mental as well as physical powers in the individual. If you completely give up the desire for anything, that thing follows you, as a shadow follows a person. You no longer have to go after wealth. Wealth starts coming after you. And in its own way, it could be a danger also. It could be a temptation. So one should be cautious about it.

The Yogi who has established himself in the total renunciation of greed for anything, acquires the knowledge of past, present and future. When the Yogi is established in absolute cleanliness, both outer and inner, he becomes fit to attain God-vision. Now, he is fully qualified. There is no more any bar. So he can, without any hesitation, without any doubt, confidently carry on his struggle on concentration and meditation. Because now he is ready. The ground is ready. He has only to do the practice of concentration and meditation.

Indescribable joy, supreme happiness come through the practice of contentment. Through the power of austerity, your senses become keen and your intellect becomes sharp. Through absorbing study of spiritual scriptures, the Yogi can have a vision of his chosen aspect of his personal God. When he carries on his studies, deeply and regularly, he can have a vision of his personal God. One who studies the Bible very, very devotedly, regularly, with great feeling for a long period of time, he can have vision of Jesus. He gives Darsan. Patanjali says, perfect establishment in Isvarapranidhana itself is enough to give Samadhi. Thus perfected, if the Yogi practises Asana and Pranayama, then he becomes fit to enter into the inner aspect of Yoga, the withdrawal of the mind from the outer objects which is a discipline to be cultivated throughout the waking hours. It is not one that is done at a particular fixed time as a technique as in Asana or Pranayama or meditation.

This withdrawal you will have to practise throughout your waking hours and you have to acquire the ability even while you are amidst you normal activity. You must acquire the ability of not allowing even one per cent of your mind to go out and get involved in things and environments. You will have to acquire the habit of indrawnness in the midst of external activity. So Pratyahara is a way of life.

Pratyahara is a new habit you develop during your activities of the waking hours where you do not allow your mind to be overcome by the fascination of outer things and their allurement and attractions.

You try to retain and maintain a state of constant discrimination and wisdom by always being active in discrimination, knowing that the outer universe and its objects are passing appearances. You succeed in getting established in a habitual state of inner detachment. The mind goes out towards objects and the senses move amidst objects only to the extent absolutely essential and necessary for the purpose of fulfilling your duties and your work. Otherwise, the rest of the mind is always in a state of inwardness. This is Pratyahara. This we will take up in the next class. Hari Om Tat Sat.

Seventh Lecture: the Awakened Mind

Raja Yoga brings you the concept of a state of the mind, where you are successful in dominating in the power of wise thinking, discrimination and its power of philosophical intelligence, its power of higher, awakened rationality. It succeeds in imparting to the senses, the strength of spiritual enquiry. This is Pratyahara. The technique of this process is explained in Raja Yoga in a very interesting way that we dwelt upon last time. They say: 'To whom is the kingdom of God; it is to him who is blind though he has eyes, who is deaf even though he has ears, who is dumb even though he has tongue.' Mind should be made no mind. Pratyahara is the fifth step relevant to us in the situation of the individual, which Patanjali explains in this way before proceeding to the next higher steps. They try to gradually edge the nature of the seeker away from his love and attraction for the world appearances and take it towards the ideal. One of the practices is austerity or Tapas. It forcefully checks the outgoing nature of the senses and puts a stop to the direction of the flow of the mind object-ward, world-ward.

Tapas puts a stop to the flow of the mind object-ward and Svadhyaya tries to persuade the mind to take a new direction. So, they try somehow, to gently goad the flow of the mind higher, upward and Godward. Because, day after day, you come into living contact and communion with the inspiring and uplifting thoughts of great ones, illumined souls, master minds, and you are caught up in the power of their inspiration, you are induced and you emulate the lofty example they hold for you, through their teachings and their own personal life and example. In this way, Svadhyaya carries further the work started by Tapas. In order to enter into Raja Yoga proper, the inner Yoga which is concentration and meditation, you have to bring about a change in the direction and flow of the mind. Its flow towards appearances, towards phenomenon, towards the world, towards objects and enjoyments, should be directed towards the Reality, towards the Eternal which is Truth, that which is your goal, that great experience, that attainment which makes your life truly successful and full. This change or directing, commencing with Tapas, is furthered by Svadhyaya and when you come to Pratyahara, it is confirmed, and given a definite and a final shape through Pranayama. This state of moving upward and Godward becomes a permanent state of being in you. You become established in a state of mind or you acquire a new nature where the senses refuse to go towards sensual things, gross things, for they change their age-long habit of movement towards objects and they begin to follow the nature of the enlightened mind or awakened mind—the mind which is now endowed with a higher understanding and discrimination.

Now, you have imparted to the mind the greatest way by the practice of Yoga, company of holy people, by Yama, by Niyama and by complete change of your life. The mind having become strong, the senses tend to initiate the strength of the mind. They also go after the nature of the mind and they follow the mind. Instead of the mind being dragged by the senses, now senses follow the mind. The whole position is reversed.

When a little boy or a girl, tries to hold the leash of a big dog, the dog drags the child. But supposing it is an adult who is holding the leash, then the dog is dragged by the adult. It obeys the adult. So now, the senses become obedient. They follow the mind and this becomes the new habit pattern of the seeker. He becomes established in the state. The senses are always under the control of the higher awakened, strengthened mind, strengthened through discrimination, through Yama and through Niyama.

Among all these practices, I had occasion to mention last time that Pratyahara, unlike the other practices such as Pranayama, Trataka, etc., is not a technique to sit at a particular place and time and then practise. But it is a Sadhana which you practise during working hours, throughout your waking hours from morning till night, even when you are engaged in your activity, amongst people, amongst things, in the market, in the bazaar, in your office. You must train your mind in such a way that you give only that much of your psychic personality necessary for the job in hand. You may give the whole mind, only a confined area, the limited processes in which you are occupied. Don't allow the mind to go out of that limited area. Give the mind any process which attracts your attention in a limited way so that your mind is not dispersed. Also see that one part of the mind is always turned inward, is always discriminatory. 'Yes, I am doing this. This is not the main purpose of my existence. My goal is different. I do this because of the necessity of my secular life. Let me convert it in such a way that it is also spiritualised and becomes a part of my Sadhana, and even while I am doing this, I should not forget my goal.' So, there is an unbroken under-current of remembrance, awareness of the Reality, even in the midst of your being induced and occupied in appearances. So, this state of not giving the mind one hundred per cent out to activity but always retaining a part of it in your centre or in the Self or in God—this is Pratyahara.

Establishment In Pratyahara

In this state, the impact of experiences takes on a different nature altogether. Before, when you were totally expressing yourself to the impact of outer perceptions, each thing had the power to shake you, to disturb you and to bring out a reaction. But when you are developed in Pratyahara, perception is seen, experience is undergone, contact is made, and yet, you are continuously reacting to something else within, in the opposite direction. This reaction is now a big blow to your previous reactions. You don't react any longer as you did before you came to seek the path, unto the quest, and into Yoga. It is something this way, in the original state while you were completely, vitally involved in external perceptions and environments and experiences, now you are no longer vitally involved. You are the master, you keep on to your centre and you never lose your ground and you become a witness of things, rather than a participator in things. Your reaction to things are no longer out of your control and the difference is in this way. For instance, suppose you are taking a walk in the forest and wood-cutters are felling a big tree. As the tree crashes to the ground, if you happen to come under the impact of the branches, you will be injured. But, suppose the same thing happens in this way. They are felling a tree and you are taking a walk but you are just out of the reach of the tree. Also while you are on one side of the tree, the sun is on the other side. And as the tree crashes, the shadow of the tree falls upon you and passes over you and then the tree goes to the ground. Now, something has passed over you, something of the tree, but yet you are not affected by it at all. It has not touched you, not been able to injure you. Why, only the shadow has passed over you.

In the same way, only the shadow of all perceptions passes over the psyche of the mind and not the actual experience. The import of the actual experiences is no longer upon the inner being when one is established in Pratyahara.

There are three kinds of contacts. One is the contact of the individuals with objects, contact of the senses with the sense-objects. This is the grossest, outward form of contact in which one has not awakened even to the earliest stages of one's discipline and training. The wise masters say, you have to deny yourself this contact. You have to raise yourself from this contact. Because, you are not strong, you fly away from such objects. You place yourself in a better environment, because, you are not strong enough, you are nothing inside. Therefore, the first part of spiritual life is carefully adjusting this contact in its most crude stage. But, supposing you have come to gain certain amount of inner strength, human understanding, you have no longer any fear to have these contacts.

The second contact is of the mind with the senses. What happens is, in that stage, when you have become self-controlled, when your mind has become more enlightened, then you can afford to go amidst tempting environments, go right in the midst of objects. You take the risk, yet you are saved. Because, even when the senses come into contact with the objects, the mind refuses to take this contact in, upon itself. It says 'no'—that is the withdrawal from the second contact.

Still higher is that contact made when you are established in wisdom, established in discrimination. You are in the midst of objects, senses are contacting the objects and for purposes of your duty or due to circumstances, you have to pay attention on these and have to put your mind into them. Here, yet your ego-consciousness has not acquired an iota of desire for them, even when the mind is involved and is taking interest for specific reason, yet it says: 'I am not touched by this. Though the senses are involved in them, yet I am only an unaffected, unattached witness of these things. In my estimation they have no value. So, I am in my centre.' So, you disconnect yourself with the mind and the senses. This is the third withdrawal. You are withdrawing both the senses as well as the mind from the objects. Pratyahara is this state where you identify yourself with the reason and not with the mind, with the Buddhi and not with the Manas. This Buddhi is pure reason that which is endowed with discrimination, with greater and deeper understanding, a greater, newly found will-power. You identify yourself with that will, spiritual will and refuse to have any relationship or have any connection with even the activity of the mind within and the activity of the senses without. This is real Pratyahara. In this state, you are so able to train the mind and the senses that the eyes see but yet they do not look. Looking is a deliberate process in which you are engaged when the ego is one with the sense. 'I will not associate myself with these processes.' Though the eyes do see, you are not interested in looking. The ears hear but you refuse to listen, the tongue tastes but you are not interested in relishing. The mind thinks but you refuse to dwell upon it. This is Pratyahara. See but do not look. Hear but do not listen. Taste but do not relish.

If a student is very earnest, he does not merely want to get a degree. He is not merely interested in passing an examination or securing a particular class. But he wants not only to get a first class, but he wants to be the first student in his college, may be he wants to become the first in the whole state.

An Olympic competitor does not want to merely win a silver medal or the third position.

He wants to knock off the championship. Just as a student who wants to be first in the University, the first student in the training college and in a singe University or like a competitor who wants to be the Olympic world champion—these two people, in order to be able to keep the objective of theirs in the pursuit of their study and sport, deny themselves anything and everything which they feel, is not in accord with the all out effort of theirs. So, they cut off night clubs, they cut off parties, they cut off cocktail parties, they cut off smoking, they cut of drinking. Anything which all people like very much, desire very much, engage themselves in very much and regard as normal, they are prepared to give up. Why? Because, they had made up their minds to achieve something. It is so, in an ordinary achievement, in normal worldly life, in all engagements. For instance, the student at least tries to save time and give maximum to study. And other social engagements he cuts down, everything to the minimum. He does not go to cinema. He does not go to cocktail party or any other place of entertainment.

It is even harder with an athlete. Because, it is not only a question of utilising time in study, not distracting their attention, but also keeping the body in a perfect condition. He ousts himself from every normal thing which ordinary people take. He does not take too much starch or sugar or things which affect his health. So he forgoes many things. He is almost like a Yogi. He does not eat chocolate. He does not eat ice-cream. He does not take soft drinks. He gets up early in the morning and may be he runs with the trainer behind his motor car. In this way, he trains himself. Because, he sets as his goal to become first in whatever he undertakes. The total conquest of both your external and internal nature and to ascend into a nature of absolute mastery and perfection is the goal of the Raja Yogi. He does not want to do things halfway also. He does not want to perpetuate his problems. He does not want to keep his problems. He wants to put an end to them once and for all, so that there will be no more problem for him, no more fear, no more bondage, no more suffering. Once and for all, he wants to transcend them and master them for all time to come. So, he is prepared to face them. The extent to which one attains mastery over them is fascinating.

I have elaborated upon Pratyahara and once you have succeeded in thus changing the very direction of things from the worldward, upward and Godward, you are well set for Yoga proper. It is usual to regard these five steps, Yama, Niyama, Asana, Pranayama and Pratyahara as the outer Yoga, and Dharana, Dhyana and Samadhi as inner Yoga.

The Inner Yoga

Inner Yoga is the real Yoga. With the achievement of success in Pratyahara, the practitioner becomes fully qualified and capable of entering into inner Yoga. Concentration, therefore, becomes easy now. All the obstacles to concentration have been removed and the mind has been made a fit instrument for concentration.

Concentration is defined by Patanjali Maharshi as the localising of the mind-stuff. Localising means binding it to one place. What is that one place? The focal point of your concentration—may be an idea, may be an object, may be a figure and may be a symbol. Here, we have to understand a number of interesting things regarding mind, regarding concentration. If your efforts should smoothly progress, unhampered and be successful, the first thing is that you have to clearly understand that we have only one mind. We don't have one mind for Yoga and concentration, and another mind for gossiping and going about doing everything else in the world, so that one mind is not affected by what the other mind does. It would be wonderful if it is so, but it is not so.

So, it means, if you want to have successful concentration, you have to take care what the mind is doing rest of the time. For, at set hours, morning and evening you are trying to make the mind still, steady. Your daily life is full of processes and activity and that brings tension upon the mind. It excites the mind and stimulates it and scatters it away. Everything you are trying to do in that half an hour or one hour, morning and evening, you are trying to undo the rest of the time. Therefore, if you are really entering into Yoga, really anxious in succeeding in concentration and really sincere about it, your daily life must gradually begin to change and the pattern of its activities must gradually begin to be in harmony with concentration which you are trying to practise. If they are of two different patterns and there is disharmony between your daily patterns and concentration, you make things difficult for yourself. They must harmonise. Secondly, the mind, Prana and body are interconnected. For instance, you drink. What is the drink that starts eating your mind? It is alcohol. Do you think it will keep the mind calm after you drink? You have not opened and put it in the head, but put it in your stomach. It starts making your mind jump like a monkey. There is a connection between what is put into the stomach and the mind.

If you eat morphia, you go to sleep. This is a quick working agent and others are slow working. Your normal food in your life has an affect upon your mind and you have to learn what foods are of exciting nature or quality, and what foods are of a calming nature or quality. So, you must have the Yogic knowledge of Sattvic, Rajasic and Tamasic qualities of food. You must give up completely all kinds of Tamasic items from your diet. And you have to reduce the Rajasic type of food. Keep it in a moderation and try to make your diet largely Sattvic. This is a very important and wise thing to do. If you do it, it will help you to attain concentration.

The Master Jesus has said: "Where the love of your heart is, there the mind is." When a man is terribly in love with a woman, he need not have to be induced to think about the woman. He will always remember her. He cannot forget her. And a mother does not require to be induced to think of her child whom she loves very much.

Always her mind is there, because her heart is there. This is one of the secrets for a true, successful Yoga practice. If you love your Lord with all your heart, with all your might, with all your soul, then concentration comes like a galloping horse. But, if your love is divided, concentration is not very easy.

So, the more you develop your love for the ideal, the Atman, God, Allah, whatever it is, the more you develop intense love, hankering, great yearning, if you make that your beloved, your real treasure, your real wealth and if all other things come only second, and if that is the one thing which is first, then concentration will become easy. So, one of the secrets of success in the practice of concentration, in the practice of meditation and Yoga, is to try every means to develop greater and greater love for the Supreme, for the Divine; and here I come to a very vital thing.

What is Yoga and who is really practising Yoga? Who is really a Yogi? A Yogi is one who has decided that the goal of his life is the attainment or union with God and who has also decided to make his life a process of attaining God and who is also determined that he will practise all such things that will make this attainment as early as possible, as quickly as possible. So, he is a person who has dedicated himself for the attainment of God. So, now, whether you are in Yoga, whether you are really a Yogi, you try to find out by asking yourself this question: 'What is the one dominant passion of my life, what is my main ambition in my life?'

Samadhi Or Superconscious State

Every year, holy Master Swami Sivananda used to give a message for his Birthday. We used to call it a Birthday message. Each year, the Birthday message had a heading. In one year, the heading was

"God First, the World Next and Yourself Last." This was the heading of the message: God first, the world second and yourself last, if at all. That means, that the essence of his message was "O man, live first and foremost to attain God. And the second thing in your life—let it be service of humanity. This should be your vision and attitude. The ambition to attain God should form a dominant factor in your life. If your ambition is to attain God, all other things will take a second place. When the centre of your life is occupied with this dominant ambition to attain God-perfection, Divine experience and the others occupy the second place, then you are a Yogi. You are practising Yoga. You are on the path." This is the essence. This is also the secret of concentration and meditation. Where the love is there, the mind does not require much inducement towards it. Because, the mind follows the heart. Remember there is only one mind with which you have to do the activities of both your inner spiritual life and outer secular life. What is the quality of your outer secular life when you are engaged in concentration and meditation? These are thoughts on Dharana.

And when this localising the mind or fixing it to the point becomes continuous, unbroken, that is called meditation. Concentration and meditation are not different processes. They are not two different things. They are two phases of the self-same process. It is like water becoming snow and snow becoming ice. Snow and ice are not two different things. When cold becomes continuous and more intense, water freezes. So, when this fixing of the mind to one point becomes continuous and unbroken, you gain concentration. Concentration leads to meditation. And, as meditation takes on great intensity and depth, a certain blessed moment comes when suddenly the door-ways of intuition are opened, the eyes of intuition are opened up and we enter into a transcendental experience. *This is Samadhi. This is the goal of Yoga.*

When the spiritual consciousness suddenly dawns, you are no more in the level of either the body or the mind. It no longer thinks through the mind. Consciousness becomes your experience and not thought. You rise beyond the mental plane and enter into the spiritual plane, spiritual experience. The dawn of spiritual consciousness brings about the ultimate transcendence of all mental experiences, human experiences, sorrow, grief, anxiety, suffering, doubt, restlessness and pain. They are left behind. It is like one having attained a mountain top. When you were approaching the foot of the mountain in order to climb up, you had to struggle through great jungle, forest, towering trees, thorny bushes, and so you had great difficulty in making progress, making clear a path through the thorny bushes and obstacles and reach the foot of the mountain and start climbing. And when you reach the peak, that in which you were caught and through which you were looking at the top, the towering trees, big creepers and thorny bushes, now they become like a dimensionless green carpet. They no longer tower above you. They are levelled. You are towering above them and they look like a carpet as though they have no height at all. So the whole relationship is changed.

All human experience is only mental experience. Everything the human being experiences is in the mind only. When you enter into the transcendental state of spiritual consciousness, all mental experiences, all human experiences are left behind, and you enter into Divine experience. From that ground of Divine experience, these lower experiences look like children's play, forgotten dreams from which you have awakened. You rejoice now, and no more sorrow, no more fear, no more worry, and no more grief. That is Samadhi. That is your goal. That is awaiting you. That is your birthright. Ask and it shall be given. Seek and you will find. Knock and it shall be opened unto you. So, do you want that experience, or you want to continue in your same weeping and wailing, laughing and crying, ever restless, ever discontent? It is for you to decide.

The Supernatural Powers

I conclude this evening after reading a fascinating chapter in the Patanjali Yoga Sutras. I read rapidly the Sutras of this chapter in English, so that it gives you an idea of one who has completely entered into the practice, this inner mastery and what type of outer mastery comes to one spontaneously. It is through this inner mastery and the resultant outer mastery, that the ancients in the East were able to do incredible things, which, to do now, we have to spend millions and billions of dollars. For example, we have tried to get the knowledge of outer space by incredibly costly instruments, and yet it is still a hypothesis only, though to some extent, we have sure knowledge also. Based upon that knowledge we are able to predict many things.

But, how those people predicted it? How did those ancients, who did not have physical laboratories or the modern instruments, achieve many astounding things? How are they in the East able to chart the course of the stars? How are they able to predict to the minute, to the second, each and every lunar and solar eclipse, the tides and the movements of the entire heavenly bodies? How they are able to do it? It has been going on in India for thousands of years. We have what is called our Panchanga, the almanac, and every new year the almanac is published. In the almanac is given accurately to the second, at what time the solar eclipse will begin and when it will reach its middle point and at what minute it will end. And they do it at the beginning of the year. How are they able to do it? What are their methods? And they knew also what is moving and what is not moving. They had no superstitions about that exact knowledge. And as you go through this, you get some knowledge, some idea of how they might have got this knowledge without any instrument. How do they get these powers?

Patanjali says, you can get the absolute knowledge of anything in this universe, if you make Samyama upon it. The triple process of concentration, meditation and intuitional vision, when these three are combined, it is called Samyama.

You make Samyama upon water, you know everything about water. You make Samyama upon wind, you know everything about wind. You make Samyama of fire, you know everything about fire and the moment you know everything about it, you gain mastery over it. Now, fire cannot burn you. In this way, Samyama is the secret. The Yogi who has attained the highest stage of Yoga by making Samyama on the three kinds of changes, obtains the knowledge of the past, present and the future. By making Samyama of the source of the word, one obtains perception of a meaning, understanding of all kinds of sounds, utterances of all living beings. If you do Samyama upon the sound of a word, then you are able to understand the meaning of what the bird says, what the animal says. You can understand the language of all living creatures.

By making Samyama of previous thought-waves, one obtains knowledge of the past birth. Any perception immediately puts an impression in your mind of that you have seen, and this impression creates a thought and the thought occupies the mind and subsides. When a thought-wave subsides, it remains in the mind in a seed form, in a subtle form. Therefore, if you do Samyama upon the mind, these submerged thoughtwaves, you can always rely upon them. It means, if you do Samyama upon the thoughtwaves or impressions created in this birth, you can receive your memory right up to infancy from the mother's womb. If you carry this Samyama deeper and deeper, you revive thought-waves, the impressions that have been put into the mind-stuff even in previous births and you get a memory of past births.

By making Samyama upon the distinguishing marks of another body, one obtains the knowledge of that person's mind. Because, the body is the product of the mind. The face is the index of the mind. So, if you are able to do Samyama on the form of another person, you will obtain the knowledge of the state of the mind of that other person, but not of its inner activity. If, for instance, you do Samyama upon the figure of Jesus, a time will come, you will be able to understand the mental state of Jesus. Similar is the case with Samyama on Buddha or any one.

If one makes Samyama on the form of one's own body, one can obstruct its perceptibility and separate its power of manifestation from the eyes of the beholder; then one's body becomes invisible. Because, the body is reflecting light-rays and these light-rays enter into the eyes and fall upon the retina of the person who is seeing. Thus your body becomes visible to him. If you are able to make Samyama upon the body, you are able to obstruct this perceptibility. If you are able to cut off this perceptibility of the body, you can be in the crowd of hundreds and thousands of people, and yet remain invisible to them. That is the result of Samyama on your body. So, you may be there, you may become suddenly invisible. The sounds of the body also can be silenced.

By making Samyama on the two kinds of Karma, viz., those that are to be fructified quickly and those that will bring fruits slowly at a later date, the Yogi gets the knowledge of the time of his death.

By making Samyama upon any virtue, friendliness, compassion, etc., one develops maximum powers of these qualities. If you make Samyama on a diamond, your body can become as hard as a diamond. No weapon can cut it. One can do Samyama upon an elephant and one may acquire the strength of an elephant.

By making Samyama on the inner light, one obtains the knowledge of all that is subtle, hidden or far, distant.

All this treasure of knowledge comes to one whose mind is spontaneously enlightened through purity. Patanjali also says that when the mind has reached a very high state of purification, the psychic powers detailed above may come to one spontaneously without making any kind of Samyama. This explains the miraculous powers of some of the saints who did not do any particular kind of Samyama, but surrendered to God and prayed to God and filled themselves with absolute devotion to God. They became dead to themselves and Grace came and due to their very life of purity, all types of things happened through their person.

The power of enjoyment arises from a failure to discriminate clearly between the Atman and Buddhi-sattva or the pure intellect. The intellect is merely the agent of the Atman and has independent existence only for its own sake. Therefore, making Samyama on

the distinction between Buddhi and the Atman, one gets the ultimate knowledge of the Atman. One gets enlightenment and obtains super-natural powers of hearing, touch, taste and smell through the knowledge of the Atman.

These are powers of the worldly state. All these powers pertain to the universe. But they are obstacles to the highest Samadhi. When the bonds of the mind caused by Karmas, have been loosened the Yogi can enter into the body of another by the knowledge and operation of the nerve-currents. By controlling the nerve-currents which govern the lungs and upper part of the body, the Yogi can walk on water, sharp thorns and similar objects. Or he can give up his life at will. By controlling the powers that govern Prana, he can surround himself with a blaze of light.

I just only read it to you, because it is of some interest to you to know what the Yoga text says about the possibilities of human nature.

Radiant Immortal Self! Let us thank the Divine, for He has given us this grand opportunity during the past weeks to study this science of inner discipline, training and mind-mastery. Raja Yoga is essentially the science of meditations. Just as Karma Yoga is the science of spiritualising one's activities so that it becomes connected with the Divine, and Bhakti Yoga is a spiritualisation of sentiments and emotions so that they become connected with the Divine, and Jnana Yoga is the spiritualisation of one's powers of intellect and reasoning, so that they become the instrument of connecting themselves with the Divine, in the same way, Raja Yoga is the way of spiritualising in that direction the nature or quality of the mind, the thought-force, so that it becomes the medium, the means of connecting yourself with the Divine. So, Raja Yoga is essentially the science of meditation and this has been a gift to us, the grace of the Divine.

Scriptures, teachers, teachings—all these can create interest, induce and help and inspire, but one has to utilise all the factors and start living the life and enter into the practice, and this I wish for you all and pray. Thank you for your continued interest which has made me visit here and conduct these classes, very rewarding to me and highly satisfying. May the choicest blessings of the Almighty ever be upon you all. May Master Swami Sivananda's Grace and blessings be upon you all. May your mind be propitious. May your own mind be receptive and positive, eager to take up the quest and attain fruition in it. Ultimately it is a matter of each one's choosing this path and eagerness and willingness of the mind to enter into this quest and move towards the Goal.

Printed in Great Britain
by Amazon

36396152R00088